This has not been a good time for liberals. Across the globe various liberal-based political parties have been suffering electoral downturns and loss of core support. That is why it is refreshing to read Matthew Kalkman's New Liberalism, both because of his obvious commitment to liberal principles but also because he puts a new liberal lens on contemporary issues.

I was particularly struck by his strong case for liberals to take on the cause of freedom for future generations, what he calls a "timeless" concept of freedom. The corollary to that concept is the need for a more creative, innovative state that defines its powers in relation to global, cross-border issues — climate change and terrorism.

This is certainly a book to be read by those who still are motivated by a liberal sensibility and want to engage in the renewal of liberal policy and practice in a global environment.

— Honourable Lloyd Axworthy, PhD
Former Minister of Foreign Affairs — Canada
Nobel Peace Prize nominee for leadership
in the global effort to outlaw landmines
Past-Director of the Liu Centre for the Study of Global Issues,
University of British Columbia
President of the University of Winnipeg

Kalkman's concept of timeless freedom is of much interest to all who want an effective state characterized by free, empowered citizens who have the possibility to shape their own futures. The state must make the pursuit of happiness a possibility, but not a guarantee. Liberalism brings together the free market on the one hand and free society — civil liberties, human rights, the rule of law, and democracy — on the other. They are different sides of the same coin and cannot be separated. New Liberalism builds upon this idea. It is a must read.

— Hans van Baalen
President of Liberal International,
the World Federation of Liberal parties
Member of the European Parliament
representing the Netherlands

Broad in scope, this clearly written short book offers a strong defense of the need for a more defined and updated concept of "positive freedom" and describes an intriguing framework for the role of the state in supporting rights and responsibilities that, crucially, extend to future generations. It has a nice review of classical liberalism and social liberalism with a well-articulated framework for what "New Liberalism" ought to offer.

I particularly appreciate the attention paid to the issues posed by climate change, fiscal irresponsibility and global inequality — these are probably the most important challenges in our world today, along with the need for better governance.

— Dr. Anne M. Pearson
Granddaughter of Lester B. Pearson,
former Prime Minister of Canada
Professor at McMaster University
Chair of the Hamilton Interfaith Group

New Liberalism

NEW
LIBERALISM

MATTHEW KALKMAN

GRANVILLE ISLAND
PUBLISHING

Library and Archives Canada Cataloguing in Publication

Kalkman, Matthew, 1988-
    New liberalism / Matthew Kalkman.

Includes index.
ISBN 978-1-926991-04-7

    1. Liberalism. I. Title.

JC574.K35 2011   320.51'3   C2011-902251-6

Editors: Gordon Thomas and Kyle Hawke
Indexer: Renee Fossett
Cover and Text Designer: Omar Gallegos

Granville Island Publishing Ltd.
212–1656 Duranleau St. Granville Island
Vancouver BC, Canada, V6H 3S4

604 688 0320 / 1 877 688 0320
info@granvilleislandpublishing.com
www.granvilleislandpublishing.com

First Published in 2011
Printed in Canada on recycled paper

To my parents
Peter and Bonnie
in love and gratitude

CONTENTS

INTRODUCTION

People in contemporary liberal democracies have more freedom of choice than ever before. In the 21st Century, free markets are the norm, men and women share greater equality, health care and education are supported by governments, human rights are accepted as universal and more people are allowed to practice their own faith without persecution from the government. It can be argued that at the beginning of the 21st Century, social liberalism has emerged as the prevailing political philosophy. The beginning of this millennium brought forth new challenges and new opportunities. These challenges and opportunities demand a new liberalism — a liberalism that can tackle the problems of climate change, financial crises and global inequalities.

Exactly one hundred years after L.T. Hobhouse (1864–1929), professor at the London School of Economics, helped lay the foundations of social liberalism in his seminal work entitled *Liberalism*, we are entering the next major shift in the political dynamic. The times call for New Liberalism.

The defining features of the different classifications of liberalism are the different notions of freedom around which each revolves. Classical liberalism is built around the concept of negative freedom. This means the role of the state is to ensure freedom from harm. Social liberalism, conversely, is founded upon the concept of positive freedom, which is the freedom to develop oneself. Neither philosophy ensures these freedoms will be extended to future generations threatened by climate change, fiscal irresponsibility and global inequality. To tackle these challenges, a new concept, one of 'timeless freedoms' is needed.

The relationship between liberalism and the role of the state has always been defined by two pillars — the notion of freedom and the social contract of the time. In *New Liberalism*, the social contract is defined as the amount of power the individual is willing to tolerate in the hands of the state. The social contract has shifted throughout time, along with two tensions which have served to define the role of the state. Horizontal tension exists between states and the market. Vertical tension pulls power down to the individual as well as up to the global level.

Horizontal tension exists between the state and the market, the question being which has the most power. Historical examples include planned economy versus free market economy and a regulated versus unregulated marketplace. Vertical tension pulls power down to the local level and up to the global level. Examples of power being devolved to the individual include human rights and the growth of civil society. Examples of power being extended to the global level include the growth of institutions such as the United Nations and the European Union. The shocks of the financial crisis of 2008 that started with the collapse of the housing market in the United States have resulted in new discussion about the relationship of state and market, calling into question the unyielding ability of markets to solve all problems. What is *not* called for is a return to big state involvement. Rather, a state that is smarter and more effective than it has been previously should establish more innovative relationships with markets, civil society and global institutions.

The pillars of timeless freedom and a new social contract inform the modern state as to its role in the world. The concept of timeless freedom makes it a necessity for the state to not only defend the freedoms of the people presently living in it, but to ensure the freedoms of future generations. Within this reformulated structure, the state still has a positive role to play in the modern world. The state will not only focus on protecting the freedoms of the future but also has a continued obligation to extend freedoms within itself, as well as extending freedoms beyond the state. These are included in essential services and advancement of multicultural policies. Beyond its borders, the state must take action on genocide, terrorism, nuclear disarmament and disease.

Understanding the evolution of liberal thinking is fundamentally important to understanding the process within liberalism of modernizing itself to constantly expand freedom as befits the times. The two major forms of liberalism — classical and social variants — shall be examined prior to embarking on the purposes and values of New Liberalism. To assess classical and social liberalism, the concept of freedom must first be assessed, followed by the social contract that traditionally accompanied this freedom, then the role of the state that flows from the merging of the two. The evolving role of the state will itself be shown to be defined by the actions taken by political leaders who either self-identified as liberal or took actions that focused on increasing individual freedom in either a classical or social sense.

The idea of New Liberalism is founded upon the ideals and freedoms we have fought for and enjoy today which need to be extended and responsibly protected for future generations, a concept of timeless freedom. This requires a more creative, more innovative and more dynamic state than has ever existed — one that works with markets, civil society and global institutions in a more sophisticated manner. It also requires a state that can tackle problems individuals cannot tackle by themselves. With the implementation of New Liberalism, the challenges of the 21st Century can begin to be addressed.

New Liberalism should not be viewed as a political manifesto or policy booklet. Rather, it should be seen as a framework that will modernize liberalism to face the challenges we are now experiencing at both local and global levels. At the heart of New Liberalism is the central philosophy that freedoms, in both the negative and positive sense of the word, need to be extended to future generations.

1

CLASSICAL LIBERALISM

"No one ought to harm another in his life, health, liberty, or possessions."[1]

With these words John Locke (1632–1704) founded the thinking that would instigate revolutions, overthrow monarchs and ultimately bring the greater equality, freedom and opportunity that defines the world we live in. From this starting point, liberalism has had a long struggle to make its way forward. It has fought off fascism and communism, socialism and conservatism. Through this process, liberalism itself has evolved in order to tackle the challenges of the times. Classical liberalism directly defined the role of the state for over a century based upon the two pillars of negative freedom and the social contract.

The first pillar, negative freedom, signifies freedom from harm and is composed of both rights and responsibilities. In the original conception of classical liberalism, John Locke proposed the notion of natural rights. This was born out of the desire to counteract the idea of the Divine Right of Kings by declaring that rights belong to every individual, rights which even the monarchs could not overturn.[2] This notion completely altered the structures of power that came before. This vision has evolved into our modern concept of human rights. The original conception of natural rights aligns

---

1 Locke, J., *The Two Treatises of Civil Government* (Hollis, 1689): 289.
2 Locke, J., *The Two Treatises of Civil Government* (Hollis, 1689).

with the first generation of the three generations of rights theory proposed by Karel Vasak,[3] discussed later in this chapter.

Integral to the concept of natural rights is the principle of responsibility, for freedom entails rights and responsibilities both. The responsibility of classical liberals was defined most explicitly by John Stuart Mill (1806–1873) and his harm principle,[4] centred on the idea that individuals should be free except where they cause harm to others and the government should confine itself to intervening only in those situations where harm is incurred. The harm principle defined the responsibilities of individuals and the government in how they should function in their respective spheres. In the book *On Liberty,*[5] Mill puts forth "That the only purpose for which power can be rightfully exercised over any member of a civilized community, against his will, is to prevent harm to others."[6] This harm principle will be shown to be an important foundation to the argument of timeless freedoms.

Mill stated that all of his books were co-written with his wife Harriet Taylor Mill (1807–1858). He declared that "when two persons have their thoughts and speculations completely in common it is of little consequence in respect of the question of originality, which of them holds the pen" and in a letter to her in 1854 acknowledged that "I shall never be satisfied unless you allow our best book, the book which is to come, to have our two names on the title page. It ought to be so with everything I publish, for the better half of it all is yours."[7] Therefore, *On Liberty* should truly be described as a joint work, though that is often forgotten.

The second pillar, the social contract, is defined as the power given to the state by the people governed. This is composed of a

---

3 Vasak, Karel, "Human Rights: A Thirty-Year Struggle: the Sustained Efforts to give Force of law to the Universal Declaration of Human Rights," *UNESCO Courier* 30:11, (Paris: United Nations Educational, Scientific, and Cultural Organization, 1977).

4 Mill, John Stuart, *On Liberty* (London: Longman, Roberts & Green, 1859).

5 Mill, John Stuart, *On Liberty* (London: Longman, Roberts & Green, 1859).

6 Mill, John Stuart, *On Liberty and Utilitarianism. Bantam Classic Edition* (New York: Bantam Dell, 1993 [1859]): 14.

7 Mill, John Stuart, *Autobiography.* vol.1, ed. J. Robson and J. Stillinger (Toronto: Toronto UP, 1981): 251.

horizontal negotiation of powers between the state and markets and the vertical tensions of power arising from both a local and global level. With regards to the negotiation of powers between the state and the markets in this era, there was a focus on laissez-faire economics and a minimalist state, which was bolstered through the works of Adam Smith (1723–1790).[8] However, it was the vertical negotiation of powers that truly altered the shape of society as its focus was no longer on the monarch but on the individual. This in turn led to calls for the monarchy itself to have its powers limited by a constitution.

The original proponents of liberalism saw it as a tool for freedom and one that focused on certain core ideas. Central to their notions was the idea that humans were rational self-interested individuals who had natural rights, including the right to property. These rights were always seen in a negative sense, in that they were meant to prevent people from being subjected to actions of others. Going hand-in-hand with these ideas were free markets, free trade and limited government. The freedom that classical liberalism is founded upon is the idea of negative freedom, where its social contract focused largely on a free market and a minimalist state. This reduced the role of the state to helping open free markets and free trade, as well as limiting its own activities to stopping people from harming others. The role of the state under classical liberalism will be examined by assessing the actions of the liberal governments of the period.

NEGATIVE FREEDOM

The cornerstone of classical liberalism has been the philosophy of negative freedoms. It is from this concept that the traditional form of 'hands off' government extends. The concept of negative freedoms first became defined as separate from positive freedoms by Isaiah Berlin (1909–1997) and his *Two Concepts of Liberty.*[9]

---

8 Smith, Adam, *The Wealth of Nations*, ed. *R.H. Campbell, A.S. Skinner, and W.B. Todd* (Oxford: Clarendon Press, 1976).
9 Berlin, Isaiah (2002) *"Two Concepts of Liberty," Four Essays on Liberty.* (Oxford: Oxford University Press, 1969).

The concept itself can be traced back to Thomas Hobbes (1588–1679) and the father of classical liberalism, John Locke. Thomas Hobbes defined it as follows: "a free man is he that in those things which by his strength and wit he is able to do is not hindered to do what he hath the will to do."[10]

As previously stated, natural rights have served as an integral part of the concept of negative freedom and it is important to understand the relationship between natural rights and the key liberal value of human rights. One thing must be clear about these natural rights — they were only considered in their negative sense. They were largely a reaction to the Divine Right of Kings, by saying all humans are born with rights and are not merely born to be subservient to a king.

The concept of natural rights is inextricably linked with the concept of human rights, albeit in negative form. This is often equated with first-generation rights of the three generations theory of human rights proposed by Czech Jurist Karel Vasak.[11] The three generations of rights were meant to roughly correlate with the French motto of 'liberté, égalité, fraternité'. First-generation rights are most closely related to civil and political rights. Now codified in the International Convention on Civil and Political Rights and the Universal Declaration of Human Rights, these rights are essentially in place to protect the individual from the state and are inclusive of such concepts as the right to freedom of speech and freedom of religion.

These rights first found form in the United States Bill of Rights and the French Declaration of the Rights of Man and of the Citizen. Correlating the traditional notion of natural rights with these codified legal human rights would place them within the first generation of rights. Attached to these rights is a sense of responsibility. The major underlying principle of negative freedom,

10 Hobbes, Thomas, *Leviathan* Second edition. (London: George Routledge and Sons, 1886 [1651]): 100.
11 Vasak, Karel, "Human Rights: A Thirty-Year Struggle: the Sustained Efforts to give Force of law to the Universal Declaration of Human Rights," UNESCO Courier 30:11, (Paris: United Nations Educational, Scientific, and Cultural Organization, 1977).

the harm principle, is fundamentally important to understanding negative liberty because it describes the role of the social contract and the role of the state. John Stuart Mill said "the only purpose for which power can be rightfully exercised over any member of a civilized community, against his will, is to prevent harm to others. His own good, either physical or moral, is not sufficient warrant."[12] Furthermore, he said, "Over himself, over his own body and mind, the individual is sovereign."[13] Even though the language discussed in this early period was about rights, what is inherent in the harm principle and in the social contract is the idea responsibilities do exist. This is important to remember. Often liberalism gets caught up in talk of rights but belonging to the social contract requires a responsibility to society be recognized as well. More and more, societies are recognizing that with rights come responsibilities. The original form of responsibility demanded of liberals was a responsibility to ensure one does not harm another.

Above all, it is this notion of negative freedoms that has served as the basis of classical liberalism. As was stated previously, the power of this concept caused empires to be overthrown, old ideologies to be thrown out and a new structure to take over — a structure that now dominates the globe. It was also this concept of freedom, along with the social contract of the time that directly influenced the role of the state at that time.

CLASSICAL SOCIAL CONTRACT

The second pillar that defines the relationship between classical liberalism and the role of the state is what is termed the classical social contract. At the heart of the social contract is the idea of the negotiation of powers, with the original contract proposing a strong role for the market and a weak role for the state. The power

---

12 Mill, John Stuart, *On Liberty and Utilitarianism. Bantam Classic Edition* (New York: Bantam Dell, 1993 [1859]): 14.
13 Mill, John Stuart, *On Liberty and Utilitarianism. Bantam Classic Edition* (New York: Bantam Dell, 1993 [1859]): 14.

struggle between markets and the state has been at the heart of the social contract since the beginning. Outside of this horizontal negotiation of powers, there was a vertical shift in power, with the individual being placed as the focus rather than the state. The philosophical foundations of the social contract will first be looked at before analyzing the state-market relationship and then turning to the accumulation of power with the individual, at the expense of the traditional view of the state. Varying accounts have existed as to the traditional purpose of creating a social contract. Most have traced it to the idea that without such a contract one would go back to the traditional state of nature. In this natural state, Thomas Hobbes argues that life would be "nasty, brutish, and short" as pure freedom would lead to a "war of all against all" (*Bellum omnium contra omnes*).[14] John Locke's idea differed from Hobbes' concept of the social contract. Where Hobbes argued that a sovereign was still needed, Locke argued that people left to their own devices would pursue the common good and would therefore make the best decisions.[15]

Jean-Jacques Rousseau (1712–1778) presented a differing social contract yet again, in the sense that Locke argued the social contract was decided by the individual, whereas Rousseau argued that the 'general will' governed the social contract.[16] This is therefore based upon a concept of popular sovereignty whereby the collective will takes precedence over the will of the individual. The idea is that the social contract can be altered by the 'general will', which is why it has been possible to have different social contracts throughout history. This is also why the possibility existed for social liberalism to have two general forms, based upon the will of the people. Rousseau still believed the general will could not equate with tyranny because it could not override the natural rights of individuals.

---

14 Hobbes, Thomas, *Leviathan* Second edition. (London: George Routledge and Sons, 1886 [1651]): 94.

15 Locke, J., *The Two Treatises of Civil Government* (Hollis, 1689).

16 Rousseau, Jean-Jacques, *The Social Contract, or Principles of Political Right* (1762).

Arguably, under the philosophy of classical liberalism, the social contract wanted a market described as a laissez-faire economy. This form of economy is essentially one where the people are best left to their own devices, with no government involvement. Fundamental components of the free market economy will set the correct price merely by allowing individuals to demand whatever is necessary, leading to equilibrium with supply. This is as opposed to the planned economy, which revolves around the idea that the state should control the means of production so as to best produce the most humane economy. One of the earliest schools of economy, preceding Adam Smith, was Physiocracy.

Physiocrats essentially were of the view that it should be productive work that would be measured and not mercantilism which was based upon the wealth of the monarch. The weakness of their idea was its focus on agriculture. The Physiocrats really put the foundation down for what was to become classical political economy. It was François Quesnay (1694–1774), the head of the Physiocratic movement who proposed the wealth of a nation came from its production and not from its collection of rare metals.[17] Adam Smith said of the system espoused by the Physiocrats, "with all its imperfections [perhaps] the nearest approximation to the truth has yet been published upon the subject of political economy."[18]

Out of the explosion of knowledge resulting from the Scottish Enlightenment arose the arguments of Adam Smith who laid the foundation of the first true economic philosophy and the concept of classical political economy. The foundation of a market society is the idea that goods and services should be priced based upon supply and demand. Smith's essential argument was based around the notion that human beings left to their own self-interest without state involvement would produce the most beneficial

---

17 Quesnay, F., "Tableau économique," (1759) from Spiegel, Henry William The Growth of Economic Thought, Revised and Expanded Edition (Duke University Press, 1983): 189.

18 Smith, Adam, The Wealth of Nations, ed. R.H. Campbell, A.S. Skinner and W.B. Todd (Oxford: Clarendon Press, 1976) vol. 2b: 678.

outcomes. In *The Theory of Moral Sentiments,* he laid out the basis of interactions between rational self-interest and unregulated markets.[19] Along with the idea of political freedoms came economic freedoms.

In his famous work, *The Wealth of Nations,* Smith made his argument about the 'invisible hand', essentially equating to the idea self-interest will better determine price by demand than could an outside force. Smith once wrote that, "By pursuing his own interest [the individual] frequently promotes that of the society more effectually than when he really intends to promote it."[20] Therefore, the invisible hand of the market does its job. "It is not from the benevolence of the butcher, the brewer or the baker we expect our dinner, but from their regard to their own self-interest. We address ourselves, not to their humanity but to their self-love and never talk to them of our own necessities but of their advantages."[21] This idea also existed in the work of a Finnish parliamentarian, Anders Chydenius (1729–1803), who was one of the first to propose free trade and unregulated industry in *The National Gain* in 1765. The writings of Rev. Thomas Malthus (1766–1834) and David Ricardo (1772–1823) furthered this fundamental economic belief that the markets would correct themselves.

This altered relationship between the state and market was matched by an alteration in the relationship between the individual and the monarch. The concept of the social contract has defined history for the last several generations, as it turned traditional relations on their head. Where originally the concept of governance was the monarch having absolute power, it was now seen with the individual being at the centre. The individual is part of a contract with society whereby certain rights are given up, in return for gaining security and protection of property among other things.

---

19 Smith, Adam, *The Theory of Moral Sentiments,* ed. D.D. Raphael and A.L. Macfie, vol. 1 of *The Glasgow Edition of the Works and Correspondence of Adam Smith* (Indianapolis: Liberty Fund, 1982 [1759]).

20 Smith, Adam, *The Wealth of Nations,* Third Edition (Hartford: Lincoln and Gleason, 1804): 349.

21 Smith, Adam, *The Wealth of Nations,* Eleventh London Edition (Hartford: Cook and Hale, 1818) vol 1: 11.

This alteration to making it about the individual flipped relations on its head. Enough cannot be said about the importance of this concept — this put the individual in the driver's seat. The reversal of power in both its political and economic sense of freedom would have the outcome of altering government from one of oppressor to one of a protector of individual liberty, only existing based on the consent of the people it governs. Charles de Secondat (1689–1755), Baron de Montesquieu, stated in *The Spirit of the Laws* that "Better is it to say, that the government most conformable to nature is that which best agrees with the humour and disposition of the people in whose favour it is established."[22]

There was no pull to the global level at this time, as it was still generally following along the lines of the Peace of Westphalia in 1648 where the state was the highest unit of governance in the world. The Peace of Westphalia consisted of two treaties that were signed in Osnabrück and Münster, which ended the serious fighting of the Thirty Years War and the Eighty Years War. This laid out the concept of Westphalian sovereignty whereby no outside actor could interfere with the territory belonging to that state and has contained powers at the state level from that time.

With regards to the power of the state at the time, principally the role of the state was now seen to be one that required the consent of the people for its existence. Its role would now only extend as far as the general public allowed it to, in contrast to the concept of absolutism, whereby the monarch has all of the power regardless of the wishes of the common man and woman. Under this view, the state was meant to be as minimalist as possible, a night watchman state with a strong free market. Furthermore, the state's powers were meant to be limited by the constitution.

A cornerstone of the new role of the state, under the liberal view, is that it will be bound by a constitution. This does not only limit the power of the state but is also used to extend and protect freedoms of all people within the state. The concept of legal codes extends in history far before liberalism came into existence.

---

22 de Secondat, Charles, Baron de Montesquieu, *The Spirit of the Laws,* ed. David Wallace Carrithers (Berkley: University of California Press, 1977 [1748]): 104.

In fact, codes of justice have been shown to extend all the way back to the early civilization of Sumer.

The United States Constitution served as one of the earliest forms of written constitution for a liberal democracy. Since then, governments around the world have extended and protected freedoms through national constitutions, perhaps the major tool to these ends. It needs to be pointed out constitutions have a history dating back far before liberalism as a philosophy came into existence. In the United Kingdom, this limitation of state powers is most commonly traced back to the Magna Carta and its forerunner the Charter of Liberties under Kings John (1167–1216) and Henry I (c. 1068/1069–1135), respectively. The Magna Carta laid out that there must be due process of law, under *habeas corpus*. It stated clearly, "No free man shall be arrested or imprisoned or deprived of his property or outlawed or exiled or in any way destroyed, nor shall we go against him or send against him, unless by legal judgment of his peers or by the law of the land."[23] Constitutions have also been seen as documents that protect certain rights of the citizens of a country. A very powerful statement of rights within a constitution is found in Canada, where a specific bill of rights is tied in, the Charter of Rights and Freedoms. This document includes the negative rights of the freedom of speech and religion, among others. While many countries have written constitutions, certain nations rely upon an unwritten or uncodified one, such as New Zealand or Israel.

A key debate which took place in the formative years of classical liberalism was the role of the monarch and whether its powers should in turn be limited constitutionally. Hobbes believed monarchies served as the best framework to deal with controlling humans, preventing them from reverting to their natural state of existence which would be "nasty, brutish and short."[24] Locke strongly opposed this type of thinking and addressed this point specifically in the *Two Treatises of Government*. Locke's view

---

23 Magna Carta (1215), Clause 39.
24 Hobbes, Thomas, *Leviathan,* second edition (London: George Routledge and Sons, 1886 [1651]): 64.

placed people at the centre of freedom, saying in their natural state they actually had more good in them than Hobbes thought. Where Hobbes thought a strong, authoritarian leader would be most helpful in curbing humans' natural savage instincts and desires, Locke trusted in the goodness of the individual and felt an authoritarian figure was not in any way needed. The question was whether the monarchs themselves were part of this social contract and therefore had responsibilities that constrained them as well. This is the concept of constitutional monarchy. Voltaire (1694–1778) was a supporter of this idea of the constitutional monarchy and this idea of a constitution formed the basis of the liberal democracy that would become the norm of the society we live in today. The concept of a constitution ensuring individual rights is at the heart of the concept of the liberal democracy.

The other great success story deriving from classical liberalism is the concept of liberal democracy itself. Traditionally it was held that hereditary kings were given the authority to govern as they were ordained by God. The change in thinking that all men and women were born free and equal demanded a form of government whereby all had equal say. The form of government that, as a result, extended freedom and equality to all citizens is liberal democracy. While the concept of liberal democracy extended greater powers to the local level, the Treaty of Westphalia ensured that the state was the highest governing unit at the time. This view of sovereignty held until the rise of global institutions which grew out of the ashes of war.

At the core of all of these changes was the instrumental empowerment of the individual that took place with the very concept of classical liberalism. The idea of an individual gaining power ultimately pulled power down from the state to the individual. This state of affairs called for strong economic and political freedoms in the negative sense, calling for less state involvement and a free market.

ROLE OF STATE

Moving forward from the concepts of negative freedoms and a classical social contract, the role of the state under classical liberalism was argued to be to open up free markets, enshrine and expand democracy and protect property rights. It was in this environment of social thought that two revolutions took place which shook the foundation of what came before. It was also this thinking that laid the foundation for the first republic in the modern era, the United States of America. When the country was founded, this thinking was embedded in the Declaration of Independence through the efforts of President Thomas Jefferson (1743–1826). The best way to assess the role of the state is to look at the actions of leaders of countries with a declared belief in the philosophy of classical liberalism. It is important to look at the character of the people at the forefront of the liberal movements in these countries to understand how liberalism affected their notion of the state, as well as the legislative and executive actions taken which reference classical liberalism.

The revolutions of America and France truly show the importance of leadership in the concept of liberalism. A true liberal leader is one who understands their limits and who serves with the consent of the people. While American leadership put their principles into practice, the leaders of France did not follow their principles or understand their limits in this period of time, leading to grave problems.

The American Revolution took place shortly after the French no longer posed a threat to the English colonies in British North America. At this point, the citizens of America started to become frustrated with rising taxes and the lack of electoral representation. This led to the creation of political bodies that would represent the populace. The British government saw this as a direct threat and sent in troops to shut down this local government. This action spurred the political leaders of the nation to put together the Declaration of Independence, stating the monarch and British parliament had no authority in the colonies. The nation also put in place a written constitution to ensure the freedoms of its citizens were protected. Thomas Jefferson was a staunch advocate of liberty and his policies while in government were to protect "life, liberty and the pursuit of happiness", thus ensuring a separation of church and state.[25] He sought to eliminate debt based upon a belief in minimal government, as well as seeking to ban the slave trade.

The anti-slavery movement had supporters on both sides of the Atlantic, with key members of the movement including Lucretia Coffin Mott (1793–1880), Harriet Beecher Stowe (1811–1896) and Frederick Douglass (1818–1895), a member of the American Anti-Slavery Society. A former slave and powerful orator, Douglass proved that intellectual capacity can be found among all people regardless of background, notably with his most famous work *Narrative of the Life of Frederick Douglass, an American Slave.* Many could not believe that a former slave could have written such an articulate book. The strong support of his future wife, Anne Murray Douglass (1813–1882), was notable in earning him his freedom — she helped him escape from his owners by providing him with a sailor's uniform and a part of her earnings to travel to New York. They were married eleven days later. The abolitionist movement also gained a great deal of support through Stowe's famous book *Uncle Tom's Cabin.*

Turning back to Thomas Jefferson, he followed the words of Henry David Thoreau "that government is best which governs least".[26] The laissez-faire economic system was seen most evidently as a policy of President Andrew Jackson (1767–1845). Jackson is known to have said, "As long as our government is administered for the good of the people and is regulated by their will; as long as it secures to us the rights of persons and of property, liberty of conscience and of the press, it will be worth defending."[27] Jackson further sought to eliminate the national debt based upon the same idea of having a smaller government. This revolution saw a clear match between liberal values and liberal leadership.

---

25 United States Declaration of Independence (1776): 1.

26 Thoreau, Henry David, *Resistance to Civil Government* (Civil Disobedience, 1849): 1.

27 Jackson, Andrew, *First Inaugural Address* (1829).

The French Revolution started on a similar basis of seeking greater individual freedom. There was a mixture of desperation, based upon famine and malnutrition, along with an irritation felt by the mercantile class at being ruled by those less economically powerful. Ultimately, these combined with the language of enlightenment liberal principles of individual freedom and the Declaration of the Rights of Man and of the Citizen was implemented. A constitution in 1791 turned France into a constitutional monarchy. It is fundamentally important to understand the effect the leaders of a political movement can have in either moving the ideas of liberalism forward or, conversely, destroying their whole intent. This was demonstrated as the revolution soon turned sour when the Jacobins, the radicals of the country, spurred a parliamentary coup that put Robespierre (1758–1794) and the Committee of Public Safety in control of the country. This led to the Reign of Terror, a period in time when the government would condemn any and all of its opposition to death. It has been estimated that up to forty thousand people were killed during this reign.

There were major abuses of power that showed Robespierre had not internalized what liberalism truly stands for, which is that government is only there under the consent of the people and not the reverse. Eventually with the instability of this republic, Napoleon was able to force his way into the leadership of the country. This served as the first major setback to liberalism and resulted in the formation of the Holy Alliance to oppose democracy and revolution.

The revolution in France led to similar revolutions in Spain and Latin America. We saw in Spain the rise of the political group the Liberales. Their goal was achieved in implementing the 1812 Constitution. These same struggles in Spain spread across Latin America which led to, for example, the War of Reform in Mexico, between the years of 1857 and 1861.

Within the United Kingdom, Prime Minister William Gladstone (1809–1898) served as the first true liberal leader of that country, bringing parliamentarians together around the idea of free markets and free trade. There has always been the argument put forward that the Liberal Party of the UK was really only descended from the Whig Party. In reality, the party started on its own merits, as it was founded upon this ideology of classical liberalism,[28] free markets and less government, which in England came to be known as Gladstonian Liberalism.

The true foundation of liberalism as a political unit can be argued to have come from William Gladstone — the Grand Old Man, as he was affectionately known. The Whigs were aristocrats who favoured a more powerful parliament at the expense of the crown. They triggered their own demise by broadening the enfranchisement of the middle class. Whigs and radicals then turned to the idea of free trade, finding it the best ground on which to maintain a united front. This newfound focus on free trade proved to be the basis for a new party, as a faction of Conservatives known as Peelites defected to the Liberals on the basis of such support. The Peelites defected because Robert Peel (1788–1850), Prime Minister of the UK, was a supporter of free trade and they supported repealing the Corn Laws, a protective tariff.

Gladstone, the leading Peelite and the first middle-class Liberal leader said, "There should be sympathy with freedom, a desire to give it scope, founded not upon visionary ideas but upon the long experience of many generations within the shores of this happy isle, that in freedom you lay the firmest foundations both of loyalty and order."[29] There are several examples of liberal initiatives Gladstone implemented. Gladstone was notable for seeking to limit public expenditure from £71,000,000 in 1868 to £67,000,000 in 1870 and 1871, allowing individuals to spend more freely.

Peace was another major goal, as peace meant more trade and further decreasing government expenses and, in turn, taxes. A major example of this is the Alabama Claims of 1872. These addressed the United Kingdom supplying the Confederates of America with financial and other assistance during the US

---

28 Douglas, Roy, *Liberals: A History of the Liberal and Liberal Democrat Parties* (London and New York: Hambledon and London, 2005): 1.

29 Gladstone, William, *On the Domestic and Foreign Affairs of England* (1879).

Civil War — the US sought claims for damages owing to the British intervention in the war, which Gladstone settled, enabling peace between the two nations. He also sought to change any laws that would hold back individuals from freedom of action. The Representation of the People Act 1884 extended the number of people eligible to vote.

Within Canada, a political consensus needed to be found that could rally support from many different cultures and backgrounds and unite them as a country — before the country as it is it today officially existed, there were several British North American colonies. The first to garner such support was the Reform Party — also known as the Reform movement as it was informal with much independence among its membership — that called for responsible government. Responsible government referenced the ideas of self-government and parliamentary accountability. It was this search for personal freedoms that led to rebellions led by William Lyon Mackenzie (1795–1861) in Upper Canada and Louis-Joseph Papineau (1786–1871) in Lower Canada. The first truly liberal party in what is now Canada came from Joseph Howe (1804–1873) in Nova Scotia. Beginning with a coalition built around bringing responsible government to the colonies, his political work was coupled with the discussion of political concepts in his newspaper, eventually leading to what is recognized as the first responsible government in Canada in 1848.

The first time Liberals in Canada were united as a whole and created a governing coalition that could win the country came at the hands of Prime Minister Wilfrid Laurier (1841–1919). It was the convention of 1893 that truly cemented a unique party within Canada, that truly brought all Liberals together — based on the notion of free trade. From this stage, classical liberalism was set to dominate the country for the next fifty years. Even though free trade is what united the party, it was a free trade bill drafted in 1911 with the United States that ultimately led to the defeat of the Liberals.

People sought a government that would limit itself to protecting property, protecting individuals from harm and opening up economic activity. Where their leaders understood the limits expected of them, we saw the rise of stable liberal democracies. Where their leaders did not understand the limits of their powers and did not limit the role of the state along the principles of negative freedoms and free markets, we saw the collapse of liberal democracies. From this position, classical liberalism continued its march around the globe. However, it was still to go through a major shift when it was realized that negative freedoms only presented a portion of the picture and the social contract of the time was not built to uphold what was to come. These changes led to the rise of a liberalism with a more complete picture of freedom, that of social liberalism.

2

SOCIAL LIBERALISM

We are today a fairer, more just and more equitable world because of social liberalism. We have realized the public interest is in the individual's interest. We have institutions protecting us when we have a run of bad luck, or are in need of health services. We have a smarter, more educated populace and more can now retire in dignity. Almost every successful government in this modern world follows the social liberal model balancing free markets and a welfare state. Social liberalism is itself based upon the concept freedom from harm does not truly capture the essence of freedom — to be truly free requires the freedom to develop oneself. This is why we experience calls for government intervention to open up opportunity for all so they can be truly free. This is also why every successful government maintains the functions of law and order, as well as providing essential social services. The First World War shook the foundations of liberal democracy but by the end of the war the number of liberal states had gone from three to thirteen. This war started the decline of older forms of government and sparked the ascent of liberalism. The Second World War pitted liberalism directly against fascism and the outcome was in favour of the liberals.

The two world wars and the Great Depression shook the very foundations of classical liberalism. This is when thinkers such as

L.T. Hobhouse, T.H. Green (1836–1882), John A. Hobson (1858–1940), John Maynard Keynes (1883–1946) and William Beveridge (1879–1963), among others, laid out the foundation of a new form of thinking that has come to be called social liberalism. The concept itself can be traced back to the writings of John Stuart Mill and is laid upon the foundation of positive freedoms. Positive freedoms are based in the idea that people should be free to fulfill their own potential. Social liberalism is now arguably the currently accepted role of the state.

There have been two broad eras within social liberalism. The first was based around the traditional welfare state and the second around a slimmer government that still protects essential services. At various times, social liberalism has been termed modern, or new, liberalism. Though these terms are used interchangeably, the term *social liberalism* is the most descriptive as it highlights the extension of responsibility to the community and is also the most commonly used in modern practice. Social liberalism turned to positive freedoms to describe the duties of the state. Positive freedoms, the capabilities for one to be able to develop oneself to the fullest, require an ability to have basic needs met and greater opportunities to be opened up to actually achieve individual goals. Just as with negative freedom, positive freedom entails rights and responsibilities. The rights are seen to be second-generation positive rights, as part of the three generations of rights theory previously described. The responsibilities entailed individuals embracing a sense of duty to other citizens in the community to ensure the continuance and extension of these freedoms to all members of society.

Tied to this vision of freedom is the concept of equality of opportunity. Without social mobility, we aren't truly free. The idea of social mobility is that, through one's own hard work and effort, one should be able to move up the social ladder. In a free society this is possible, whereas a society is off-course when there is no potential for social mobility. Within social mobility there is a separation between intergenerational and intragenerational mobility. Intergenerational mobility applies to future generations, where intragenerational mobility means the ability for an individual to achieve success in one's own lifetime. Positive freedoms most directly relate to intragenerational mobility for reasons that relate to the concept of timeless freedom, discussed later.

John Rawls (1921–2002) had a specific viewpoint with regards to social liberalism. *On Justice* offers a justification for the redistribution of wealth, based not only on justice but what is better for individuals. Rawls demonstrates that freedom requires equality and vice-versa. He says one should start with the concept espoused by John Harsanyi of the 'veil of ignorance'. The veil of ignorance is where "no one knows his place in society, his class position or social status, nor does anyone know his fortune in the distribution of natural assets and abilities, his intelligence, strength and the like. I shall even assume that the parties do not know their conceptions of the good or their special psychological propensities. The principles of justice are chosen behind a veil of ignorance."[30] Working from behind the veil of ignorance, the average person would want a position of equality with the other members rather than chance that they would be the ones to suffer in a state of inequality. This aligns with "the principles that rational and free persons concerned to further their own interests would accept in an initial position of equality as defining the fundamentals of the terms of their association."[31] This ultimately leads to Rawls' two Principles of Justice. The first principle states that each person has an equal right to the most extensive scheme of equal basic liberties compatible with a similar scheme of liberties for others.[32] The second principle states that inequalities should only be accepted where this benefits the least well-off and that offices and positions need to be open to everyone.

The social contract altered drastically, calling for a far larger role for the state and less of a role for pure markets. The new

---

30 Rawls, J., *A Theory of Justice* (Cambridge, Massachusetts: Belknap Press of Harvard University Press, 1971): 11.

31 Rawls, J., *A Theory of Justice* (Cambridge, Massachusetts: Belknap Press of Harvard University Press, 1971): 11.

32 Rawls, J., *A Theory of Justice* (Cambridge, Massachusetts: Belknap Press of Harvard University Press, 1971): 60, 303.

concept for the role of the state was heavily interventionist. The foundations of the welfare state in the UK were laid by Prime Minister Henry Campbell-Bannerman (1836–1908) and Prime Minister H.H. Asquith (1852–1928) before the First World War with the Liberal welfare reforms. These liberal reforms focused on old age pensions and national health insurance through the National Insurance Act 1911. There was also an adoption of progressive income tax, as seen in the 1909 People's Budget. The second stage of the welfare system took place after the Second World War, based upon the ideas of the influential liberal John Maynard Keynes and of William Beveridge of the London School of Economics (LSE).

There was also another pressure at this time that pulled power from the state in a vertical direction. The power was drawn up to the global level in the form of, first, the League of Nations and, later, the United Nations. These were based upon earlier international efforts, one of which was the Permanent Court of Arbitration. A notable supporter of this idea was the peace activist Bertha von Suttner (1843–1914), who helped inspire the creation of the Nobel Peace Prize — which she herself was awarded as the first female laureate. The League of Nations was born out of the atrocities of the First World War and led President Woodrow Wilson (1856–1924) to give his "Fourteen Points" speech, which asserted that the war was being fought for just reasons. The speech was based in the idea that liberal states, just as Adam Smith first predicted, would bring about the most peaceful solution for planet Earth. We would become far too dependent on each other to start conflicts.

Another pull was from international organizations created at Bretton Woods, including the World Bank and the IMF. The very idea of the United Nations continued this liberal internationalism and the pull of power away from the state. It was the poor economic straits that people found themselves in that opened liberals' eyes to the recognition that people cannot be free without having the proper economic and political foundations in place.

In the 1970s there was a significant change in the social contract. There was a major recession and an oil crisis that shook the foundation of previous ideologies. The inefficiencies of government were starting to be seen and a renewed call for more power given to the market came about. This went hand-in-hand with calls for smaller government that took place under US Presidents Ronald Reagan and Bill Clinton, UK Prime Ministers Margaret Thatcher and Tony Blair and Canadian Prime Minister Jean Chrétien. On top of this call for more markets and less state, came a continued pull vertically, at the global level as well as the local level. This came about from the effects of globalization. This period saw a call for greater devolution of powers to the local level and a greater empowerment of the individual. This period also saw the growth of a global civil society to fill in the gaps caused by a lack of proper international structures.

At the end of the day, there have been many arguments about government-run social services but the major governments around the world are fundamentally socially liberal, protecting some form of health care service, as well as public education. One of the important factors of social liberalism was that it updated the framework of liberalism when it was needed most, when there were crises and challenges that could not be addressed through traditional approaches. This is the strength of liberalism — that it seeks greater freedom while meeting the challenges of the day. Social liberalism bolstered that strength, enhancing freedom by shifting the focus to positive freedoms.

POSITIVE FREEDOM

The concept of positive freedoms was first defined by Isaiah Berlin though it has a history dating further back. Berlin said positive freedoms were the ability " . . . to be somebody, not nobody; a doer — deciding, not being decided for, self-directed . . . conceiving goals and policies of [one's] own and realizing them,"[33] and " . . . to be conscious of [oneself] as a thinking, willing, active being,

---

33 Berlin, Isaiah, "Two Concepts of Liberty," *Four Essays on Liberty* (Oxford: Oxford University Press, 1969): 8.

bearing responsibility for [one's] choices and able to explain them by reference to [one's] own ideas and purposes."[34] Berlin further said positive freedoms were "the elimination of obstacles to [one's] will, whatever these obstacles may be — the resistance of nature, of my ungoverned passions, of irrational institutions, of the opposing wills or behaviour of others."[35]

The concept of positive freedoms extended from John Stuart Mill and Rousseau. Mill's basis for government intervention came out of the concept of utilitarianism founded by his teacher, Jeremy Bentham (1748–1832). Utilitarianism is essentially the idea of "the greatest good for the greatest number". The greatest written work on social liberalism was put forth by L.T. Hobhouse who, along with his LSE colleague John Hobson and T.H. Green, can truly claim to have laid the foundations of current liberalism.

As T.H. Green stated in an 1881 speech to the Leicester Liberal Association, "the idea of true freedom is . . . the maximum of power for all members of human society alike to make the best of themselves."[36] Green further explained:

"We shall probably all agree that freedom, rightly understood, is the greatest of blessings, that its attainment is the true end of all our efforts as citizens. But when we thus speak of freedom, we should consider carefully what we mean by it. We do not mean merely freedom from restraint or compulsion. We do not mean merely freedom to do as we like irrespectively of what it is that we like. We do not mean a freedom that can be enjoyed by one man or one set of men at the cost of a loss of freedom to others. When we speak of freedom as something to be so highly prized, we mean a positive power or capacity of doing or enjoying something worth doing or enjoying and that, too, something that we enjoy in common with others. We mean by it a power which each man

---

34 Berlin, Isaiah, "Two Concepts of Liberty," *Four Essays on Liberty* (Oxford: Oxford University Press, 1969): 8.

35 Berlin, Isaiah, "Two Concepts of Liberty," *Four Essays on Liberty* (Oxford: Oxford University Press, 1969): 17.

36 Wempe, Ben, *T.H. Green's Theory of Positive Freedom* (Imprint Academic, 2004): 111.

exercises through the help or security given him by his fellow men and which he in turn helps to secure for them."[37]

Hobhouse sought to explain social liberalism by showing that "the individual has no moral rights in conflict with the common good, as therein every rational aim is included and harmonized."[38] He went on to explain, "Thus, to the common question whether it is possible to make men good by Act of Parliament, the reply is that it is not possible to compel morality because morality is the act or character of a free agent, but that it is possible to create the conditions under which morality can develop, and among these not the least important is freedom from compulsion by others."[39]

At the foundation of positive freedom are positive rights and responsibilities. The concept of positive rights was best defined by Karel Vasak as the second generation of rights and since then, reflected in the law of many countries, building on earlier efforts. Notably, it was in fact in reaction to the Second World War that John P. Humphrey of Canada drafted the United Nations Declaration of Human Rights, codifying these human rights. The rights were further codified in the International Convention on Civil and Political Rights and the International Convention on Economic, Social and Cultural Rights. The second generation of rights has been termed positive rights, generally recognized as including the right to work and the right to housing, among others. This is because of the reaction to the Second World War and the increased understanding that such rights truly do need protection.

Freedom is created not for freedom itself but for the aiding of the development of the individual. Within the United States it was seen that:

"The process of redefining liberalism in terms of the social needs of the 20th Century was conducted by Theodore Roosevelt and his New Nationalism, Woodrow Wilson and his New

---

37 Green, T.H., *Lectures on the Principles of Political Obligation* (Batoche Books, 1883): 199.

38 Hobhouse, L.T., *The Elements of Social Justice* (H. Holt and company, New York, 1922): 40.

39 Hobhouse, L.T., *The Elements of Social Justice* (H. Holt and company, New York, 1922): 40.

Freedom, and Franklin D. Roosevelt and his New Deal. Out of these three reform periods there emerged the conception of a social welfare state, in which the national government had the express obligation to maintain high levels of employment in the economy, to supervise standards of life and labor, to regulate the methods of business competition and to establish comprehensive patterns of social security."[40]

President Theodore Roosevelt's (1858–1919) concept of New Nationalism is founded upon the idea human welfare should come before concepts such as property. This was heavily influenced by the work of Herbert Croly (1869–1930) in 1909 who wrote *The Promise of American Life*. The public strongly believed that the government could deliver social justice and so laws that opposed child labour and supported a minimum wage for women were passed. Wilson's concept of New Freedom was in direct opposition to New Nationalism and followed more along the lines of a classical liberal vision. The New Deal can be described as the birth of the purest form of government-based social liberalism. Roosevelt had a vision of Four Freedoms, three of which were liberal in the classical sense but 'freedom from want' clearly paved way for a role for government. Social liberalism was so accepted in the 1950s that Lionel Trilling (1905–1975) wrote "liberalism is not only the dominant but even the sole intellectual tradition . . . there are no conservative or reactionary ideas in circulation . . . "[41]

What made positive freedoms different from negative freedoms is that, "Positive freedom is concerned, among other things, with the ability of a person to function."[42] Going further, "a person's ability to function depends on his personal characteristics, his command over commodities and resources, the commodity and resource use made by others in his community and so on.

---

40 Schlesinger, Jr., Arthur, "Liberalism in America: A Note for Europeans" (1956) from *The Politics of Hope* (Boston: Riverside Press, 1962): 89.
41 Bloom, Alexander, *Prodigal Sons: The New York Intellectuals and Their World* (Oxford: Oxford University Press, 1986): 178.
42 Dasgupta, Partha, "Positive Freedom, Markets and the Welfare State," *Oxford Review of Economic Policy* Vol. 2 No 2. (1986): 25-36.

What are often called 'basic needs.'[43] In the end, "commodities such as basic food and shelter, medical care and sanitation facilities, are goods that are required in order that a person is capable of functioning. Whatever else he requires or wants to have, he needs these. Within bounds a person can function better, more effectively, with greater availability and use of such goods."[44]

The capabilities approach of Amartya Sen truly adds an economic voice to the philosophy of positive freedoms. A key example Sen focused on was the Bengal famine. He showed that although the people were technically free in a negative sense to survive, in reality they did not have the positive freedoms needed in order to stop from starving. Sen "sees freedom not in terms of the presence or absence of interference by others but in terms of what a person is actually able to do or to be."[45] This concept of positive freedom is still argued to be the foundation of our society today, as governments still extend their protection to health care and education at the very least.

STATE-BASED SOCIAL CONTRACT

The state-based social contract varied greatly from the contract that had come previously, with a call for a greater role on the part of the state, at the expense of markets. The state's functions themselves changed from that of night watchman, to that of being redistributors of wealth and a creator of the welfare state. The market at this time became a mixed market, adopting strongly Keynesian economics. There was also a vertical negotiation of power with a greater empowerment of the individual, countering racism and sexism in the process, ensuring that in a liberal society all people were considered equal before the law. The pull upwards was

43 Dasgupta, Partha, "Positive Freedom, Markets and the Welfare State," *Oxford Review of Economic Policy* Vol. 2 No 2. (1986): 25-36.

44 Dasgupta, Partha, "Positive Freedom, Markets and the Welfare State," *Oxford Review of Economic Policy* Vol. 2 No 2. (1986): 25-36.

45 Sen, Amartya "Food and Freedom," Sir John Crawford Memorial Lecture, Washington (1987): 3.

inspired by liberal internationalism, which led to the creation of international organizations that would help with international peace and security, as well as monetary matters. As David Harvey said about this period of time, "Both capitalism and communism in their raw forms had failed . . . The only way ahead was to construct the right blend of state, market and democratic institutions to guarantee peace, inclusion, well-being, and stability."[46]

Looking specifically at the role of the state, its functions increased drastically. The Great Depression and the fear of war reminded people we are all in this together and so it made sense to help everyone achieve the freedom to develop. This is the reason the functions of the state changed from merely preventing harm to redistributing wealth and opening opportunities for its citizens.

The first social contract to come about with this era of positive freedom was a larger role for government in helping to bring about freedom in the lives of individuals. The rise of the welfare state in the United Kingdom was largely through the efforts of Prime Minister David Lloyd George (1863–1945) who laid the foundation for insurance for both unemployment and health. This concept of the state as being focused around welfare lasted until the 1970s. During this period, government was allowed to become large and its corresponding increase in functions were widely accepted. Franklin Delano Roosevelt and the New Deal were all about having a bigger government that would help jumpstart the economy after the devastation of the depression that hit American shores. Beveridge, another liberal, started to lay the groundwork for the welfare state in the United Kingdom. It was Beveridge who stated "All people of working age should pay a weekly national insurance contribution. In return, benefits would be paid to people who were sick, unemployed, retired or widowed." The purpose of the welfare state would be to confront the great challenges of Want, Disease, Ignorance, Squalor and Idleness. The state now provides to counter all of these.

---

46 Harvey, D., *A Brief History of Neoliberalism* (University of Chicago Center for International Studies Beyond the Headlines Series, 2005): 10.

The state had a further role in applying its hand in the markets themselves. This aligned with a rise in acceptance of the concept of mixed market economies. There is no country that has a true free market and the successful markets are all mixed. It was at this time the state was geared towards trying to not repeat the Great Depression. Keynesian economics were adopted and the state was tasked to create full employment and maintain the welfare of citizens. Called 'embedded liberalism', this view would "signal how market processes and entrepreneurial and corporate activities were surrounded by a web of social and political constraints and a regulatory environment that sometimes restrained production while in other instances led the way in economic and industrial strategy."[47]

It is important to assess Keynesian Economics in light of this shift. *The General Theory of Employment, Interest and Money* was the book that truly made Keynes' mark.[48] The major message of this book was that a laissez-faire marketplace would not create full employment as originally predicted. Neoclassical economists thought employment would be reached based upon the price of labour, where Keynes argued it was in fact the aggregate demand that was the key. Aggregate demand is the amount of money spent. The state is seen to have a role in jumpstarting the economy by investing in it, while others are too timid and lack confidence to purchase goods and services at the same level as before the crisis. State interventionism in the market means that it is not purely free, but is in fact a mixed market economy. The fiscal policy initiatives of government could involve or focus on investing in public infrastructure jobs or giving tax cuts. The monetary counter-cyclical policies of government could also affect the levels of employment with changes in interest rates and money supply.

At the vertical level, power was also diffused up to the global level. This was based upon liberal internationalism as espoused by

---

47 Harvey, D., *A Brief History of Neoliberalism* (University of Chicago Center for International Studies Beyond the Headlines Series, 2005): 11.
48 Keynes, John Maynard, *The General Theory of Employment, Interest and Money* (Palgrave Macmillan, 1936).

Woodrow Wilson in his Fourteen Points. The League of Nations first truly came into existence after the signing of the Treaty of Versailles in 1919–1920. The Fourteenth Point specifically laid out the necessity of the League: "A general association of nations must be formed under specific covenants for the purpose of affording mutual guarantees of political independence and territorial integrity to great and small states alike."[49] Even though Wilson's actions were important in laying a foundation based upon this liberalism, the United States failed to sign. This is often given as a central reason for the later collapse of the institution.

The Second World War truly caused the collapse of the League of Nations. There were several foundational problems with the League of Nations. Firstly, it was composed of the victors of the First World War, which automatically created tension between the Allied States and the Axis powers. Secondly, it was directly born out of the Treaty of Versailles, which became more and more unpopular as time went on, because it laid out terms for Germany that could never be met. There was also a major problem with the concept of collective security — no nation was ready to go to war and in fact the Second World War started with Britain and France appeasing Germany.

After the collapse of the League of Nations, it seemed as if the concept of the international organization had failed. Yet, after the Second World War started to draw to a close, the major parties of the world came together to forge the United Nations.

The Charter of the United Nations was largely based upon the work done by the Commission to Study the Organization of Peace under the leadership of James T. Shotwell (1874–1965). Professor Shotwell was a Canadian-born history professor at Columbia University and President of the League of Nations Association in America. Professor Shotwell was also a member of The Inquiry, the body that set out with Woodrow Wilson and Colonel House to forge peace after the First World War. In this capacity, Shotwell helped lay the foundations of the International Labour Organization.

---

49 Wilson, Woodrow, *Fourteen Points*, Joint Session of Congress (1918).

The United Nations had a difficult time in the coming years, as the elements that would lead to the Cold War were in place and relegated the UN to a small-time player as not a lot could get done with one of the two sides vetoing. Still, this also helped forge peace during that time as it opened up a form of communication between those two countries. The UN was trapped in this position until the end of the Cold War.

The United Nations is not the only international body to have come out of the ashes of world war. There were bodies put in place to create a new economic order at Bretton Woods. The major organizations that began their life at the Bretton Woods Conference included the International Monetary Fund, the IBRD (now part of the World Bank) and GATT — the General Agreement on Trade and Tariffs (since evolved into the World Trade Organization). These institutions laid the groundwork for greater political and economic freedoms at the global level.

The World Bank is tasked with leveraging loans to developing countries and in the aim of reducing poverty. In the beginning, such loans were hard to come by as the bank wanted to protect its capacity by taking care of its own finances first. There was a major shift in thinking for the bank when the Marshall Plan was created, as it meant the European countries were able to get their financing, so the World Bank started to focus on countries outside of Europe. These loans were also infamous for focusing on infrastructure projects that would more certainly enable the loans to be repaid. When Robert McNamara took over, he aimed to invest in broader social programs, instead of simply focusing on infrastructure and public works.

The International Monetary Fund was formed for the purpose of stabilizing exchange rates in July 1944. The economic system at the time was imbalanced and corrective actions were needed. The body functions by members making contributions, which in turn are loaned to member states that have imbalances in their economic system. The IMF states it is "an organization of 186 countries, working to foster global monetary cooperation, secure financial stability, facilitate international trade, promote high employment and sustainable economic growth and reduce poverty".[50]

The GATT and World Trade Organization did not in fact start at the Bretton Woods Conference. The proposed International Trade Organization idea failed at Bretton Woods. The General Agreement on Trade and Tariffs arose to fill its place at the UN Conference on Trade and Employment. This has since evolved into the World Trade Organization. The key function of the WTO is to liberalize international trade while at the same time supervising it.

The continual pull of power down to the individual had sharply increased at this stage, resulting in more action based in the recognition that all humans deserve freedom, regardless of gender or race. The empowerment of the individual inevitably led to the conclusion all individuals should be empowered. Greater freedoms were extended during this time in the specific areas of gender and race.

Freedom at the local level requires equality in all of its senses. One of the greatest forms of inequalities that have taken place throughout history has been the inequalities of the sexes. Fortunately, women have fought for true equality to take place and the world has listened. The individual needs to be free no matter what sex they are born with and this has been recognized more and more, putting more women into the workplace than at any time in history, though there is still more to be done.

One notable example of action taken to correct the inequalities between the sexes was the struggle within Canada for women to be considered 'persons' under the law, which ultimately extended to the Privy Council in the UK with results felt throughout the Commonwealth. In modern western society, it is hard to believe a time existed where women weren't even considered 'persons' under the law — it is even harder to believe that this was within the last century. In Canada, Emily Murphy (1868–1933) set out to change this. Women at this time were not allowed to sit in the upper house of Canada, the Senate. In a system constructed to keep women out, the 'Famous Five' set out to make a fundamental

---

50 International Monetary Fund (IMF) — Mission Statement.

change which would affect common-law jurisdictions the world over — the five women fought to have women legally recognized as 'persons' under the law. This specific case did not only aim for women to be considered 'persons', it also aimed to give women the ability to sit in the upper chambers of their respective countries. At the time these goals seemed impossible, yet today are considered the bedrock of our modern society.

The case goes back to 1927, but the issue goes back even further. Emily Murphy and the Famous Five were told that they were not allowed to witness a prostitution trial. Murphy responded by complaining to the Attorney General of Alberta that "if the evidence was not fit to be heard in mixed company, then the government must set up a special court presided over by women, to try other women." The Attorney General not only agreed, but made her the first judge of a court of this type. Lawyer Eardley Jackson almost immediately challenged Murphy's appointment as she was not considered a 'person' according to common law. Though Jackson lost his challenge, it spurred Murphy to further test the waters of equality by putting her name forward for the Senate. Prime Minister Robert Borden (1854–1937) rejected her name, also citing that she was not legally a 'person' according to an 1876 common law ruling that "women were eligible for pains and penalties, but not rights and privileges." Half a million Canadians signed a petition calling for Murphy to be appointed to the Senate, but both Borden and Mackenzie King (1874–1950), Prime Minister of the next Parliament, said that though they were willing, the 1876 ruling prevented them from doing so. The Famous Five reconvened to assist Murphy in her quest to promote and establish gender equality throughout Canada. These five women signed a petition to the Supreme Court of Canada on August 27th, 1927 asking "Does the word 'person' in Section 24 of the British North America Act include female persons?"[51] The Minister of Justice submitted this reference question to the Supreme Court of Canada where it found that women

---

51 *Edwards v. Canada (Attorney General)* [1930] AC 124.

were *not* considered persons under the law. This case, known as *Edwards v. Attorney-General for Canada,* then went to the highest court of Canada, interestingly enough residing in Britain, the Judicial Committee of the Privy Council.

The presiding judge of the Privy Council was Lord Sankey (1866–1948). Sankey found that women were considered 'persons' under the law, based upon the 'living tree' principle, whereby the Canadian constitution should be read with a 'large and liberal' interpretation. This is quite an ironic citation because Sankey claimed to make Canada a "mistress in her own house" when he overruled Canada's judgment on the issue, although for the better. Following Sankey's judgment, women were finally considered persons under the law and were able to sit in the Senate. "The judgment of the Privy Council, combined with the change in political circumstances, meant that there could be no going back. Never again could anyone argue that women were not persons or could not play their full part in the public life of Britain, Canada, or any other country of the Empire."[52]

Now that the facts and the procedural history are clear, it is important to understand the reasoning behind Sankey's decision. He based his judgment on the "legal incapacity [of women]" as well as the context of public roles of women in Canada. He looked at the advances women had made by that time " . . . positions held by women more generally, and developments in property rights."[53] Sankey also found that whenever a Canadian law purposefully excluded women it did so with express words.[54] The decision in this case was that women in the Commonwealth, excluding the UK, were considered persons under the law and became eligible to sit in the upper house as long as all other qualifications are met. The reason the United Kingdom is excluded is because the case was heard in the Judicial Committee of the Privy Council, a body that

---

52 Hughes, Vivien, *International Implications of the "Persons" Case* (Canadian High Commission, London, 2000). http://www.collectionscanada.ca/04/0431_e.html, retrieved February 20 2006.
53 Riley, Maude, "Outcome — Women are 'Persons.'" http://www.famous5.org/frames/frame_education_research.htm, retrieved February 21 2006.
54 Op cit

lost its legal powers over the UK back in the 17th Century.[55] The suffragist paper *The Vote* published an article titled "Women in the House of Lords — the home country lags behind."[56] The other judgment that Lord Sankey provided in this case was that constitutions should be read as liberally as possible.

Within the greater context of the world in general, this case was fundamental in crafting recognition of the rights and freedoms of women everywhere. The most important implication it provided allowed the women of most Commonwealth countries to sit in the upper chambers of their respective countries.

Chorlton v. Lings[57] was the first case to tackle the issue of women's rights under the law within the jurisdiction of England and Wales. Its ruling is best articulated by Lord Esher, "By the Common Law of England women are not in general deemed capable of exercising public functions, although there are certain exceptional cases where a well-recognized custom to the contrary has become established."[58] The next case within the courts to affect the women's movement is *Nairn v. St. Andrew's University*.[59] This ruling stated "There can be no doubt the word 'persons' when standing alone *prima facie* includes women." It went on to say the 'persons' referred to cannot be subject to legal incapacity and, as women did not yet have the vote, they had the handicap of a legal incapacity. The vote was accordingly given to women under the Representation of the People Act of 1918. The discrimination further decreased with the Sex Disqualification Act 1919 where it said one "shall not be disqualified by sex or marriage from the exercise of any public function."

Viscountess Rhondda (1883–1958) sought to take her father's seat in the House of Lords after he passed away using the Act as support, but was told that it only removed disqualifications and

---

55 Hughes, Vivien, *International Implications of the "Persons" Case* (Canadian High Commission, London, 2000). http://www.collectionscanada. ca/04/0431_e.html, retrieved February 20 2006.

56 Op cit

57 *Chorlton v. Lings* [1868] LR 4 CP 374.

58 *De Souza v. Cobden* [1891] 1 Q.B. 687, at 691, 60 L.J.Q.B. 533.

59 *Nairn v. St. Andrew's University* [1909] AC 147.

did not create new rights.[60] Females were still not allowed to sit in the House of Lords. It was at this time that the *Edwards* case finally allowed women to be considered 'persons' under the law. This case may have had no legal effect over England but it marked the principles of *Chorlton, Nairn* and *Rhondda* as "barbarous"[61] and outdated. *Edwards v. Attorney-General for Canada* represented a great milestone in the history of women's rights. Finally, women were considered 'persons' under the law in many jurisdictions. This 'persons' status conferred equal privileges and rights to those previously enjoyed only by men. While Canada was moving forward in its rights, the United Kingdom was still in its infancy. Because of the pressures from around the world, and the citizens of the country itself, the Life Peerages Act 1958 was passed, allowing women to sit in the upper chamber, the House of Lords, for the first time. *Edwards* represents the starting point in common-law history of the deconstruction of male-oriented law. Women are now able to sit in the upper chambers, and women are now able to claim status always and forever as 'persons' under the law.

The very idea of considering women as anything but persons under the law is surprising and overwhelming to people living today. It is hard to conceive of a time when women weren't given the right to vote and weren't considered equals in society. This is why freedom is something that needs to constantly be pushed for.

This case is one example of the fight for equality that came in two waves of feminism. The first wave of feminism generally equates to women's struggle for suffrage, whereas the second wave of feminism indicated the struggle for greater rights — true equality and acceptance. The language and ideals of liberalism helped this struggle find its feet and these ideals were found through a liberal democratic system and a free market society. The concepts of political and economic freedoms have recognized equality of all people, regardless of gender, something fundamental to the current make-up of our society.

---

60 *Viscountess Rhondda's Claim* [1922] 2 AC 339.
61 *Edwards v. Canada (Attorney General)* [1930] AC 124.

Another area deeply affected by this growing empowerment of individuals was the battle against racism. The Civil Rights Movement extended directly out of this desire for greater freedoms. At the centre of the extension of freedom to all peoples, one of the most memorable events was the March on Washington for Jobs and Freedom and especially the speech delivered by Martin Luther King Jr. (1929–1968), "I Have a Dream". The power in this speech showed the power in liberalism. The freedom of speech allowed someone who was discriminated against to lay out a vision for his country that itself called for real freedom for all people — notably, the movement was named the Civil Rights Movement, signifying that it addressed the rights of all people, not of a single group.

While Canada has been held up as an exemplar of equal rights, it must be remembered that only within the last century there was a head tax on Chinese immigrants; a ship full of Hindus, Muslims and Sikhs called the Komagata Maru was turned away; there were internment camps for Japanese-Canadians; and there were various grave injustices visited upon aboriginal peoples, who were not even given the vote until 1960. A push for equality fortunately took place all across liberal democracies and ended with greater rights and greater freedoms for all citizens. This does not mean prejudice and discrimination is forgotten but it does mean that society is heading in the right direction. Ultimately, this led to Canada becoming the first country in the entire world to adopt the policy of multiculturalism, a key tenet of New Liberalism.

The magic of liberalism is that both political and economic freedoms call for equality of all individuals regardless of race or gender. A business that is unwilling to hire based upon these criteria will lose its business to other companies that are willing to open their doors, as it means the most capable people will be in the jobs.

The changes to the social contract were the most drastic swing that has ever occurred. Arising out of a philosophy of small state and free markets came a new philosophy where the state needed to be larger in order to provide the positive freedoms required for an individual to truly develop. The continual expansion of both equality before the law and freedom rapidly gained pace to provide greater rights for people of all genders and all races.

Market-Based Social Contract

Just as two world wars and the Great Depression brought about a rapid change in the social contract of the time, so did the 1970s recession and the oil crisis bring change, refocusing powers from the state to the markets. The market-based social contract has served as the basis of modern society for the last thirty years. The call has been for a decreased role for the state and an increase in the role of markets. The state morphed from being primarily a welfare state to being a regulatory state. The markets, on the other hand, started to drop the idea of Keynesianism, in favour of less state intervention.

The 1970s recession largely ended the economic boom that had taken place since the close of the Second World War. The aspect that made this recession so different was that it caused high unemployment at the exact same time as inflation was reaching higher and higher levels, known as stagflation. The root causes for this crisis are usually linked back to the oil crisis of 1973, the collapse of the Bretton Woods system and the expense of the Vietnam War in the United States. The results of this recession were shown most clearly with the stock market crash that took place from 1973–1974. The Oil Crisis was created because the world's peak oil per capita had been reached, with an Organization of Arab Petroleum Exporting Countries, or OAPEC, embargo on oil shipments to the US because of their support for Israel.

At this time there was a constant call for a smaller place for the state. The state itself had its functions changed from one primarily focusing on welfare, to one focusing on regulation. The concept of the regulatory state has, over time, turned the idea of the welfare state on its head. No longer is the government meant to redistribute wealth, but it is instead meant to focus more heavily on creating rules for society. There was a major change in functions in the state, from one of direct hands-on to a more indirect style of governance.

There was also a rise in the use of independent regulatory agencies that could not be interfered with by the political executive. This ensured a continuity of policies between parties and would bring about governance that was less politicized. It also created certain problems of its own, mainly focusing on accountability and ensuring agencies stay within their functions. The concept of the regulatory state is often attributed to Giandomenico Majone, who wrote "The regulatory state tends to favour regulation over other means of policy making. It is more a rule-making state than a taxing and spending state."[62] This landscape was drastically different from the previous welfare state. The regulatory state uses other means to achieve its outcomes. The concept of the regulatory state is really about the end of governments using power through taxation and redistribution but instead through creating rules. It is deeper than that — it also required a restructuring of how the state functions. Independent Regulatory Agencies rose which were separate from the government and made these rules. This change to the regulatory state was a necessity caused by the public desire for less top-down heavy-handed state intervention.

The market philosophy of this time was Friedrich von Hayek (1899–1992) and Milton Friedman's (1912–2006) Monetarist approach. Hayek sought a return to classical liberalism with less hands-on government. This philosophy has come to be known as neoliberalism. Attached to neoliberalism is the idea of privatization and deregulation. Privatization is the transfer of ownership of public bodies to private hands. The next phase of social liberalism came about with more calls for deregulation. The welfare state was also meant to be dismantled. What has been shown in practice is the state actually increased in size under Thatcher in the UK, Reagan in the US and Brian Mulroney in Canada, with debt exploding as well. In reality, these governments still supported the institutions founded under the previous social contract. Eventually the argument on the Conservative side would change to arguing that

---

62 Majone, G., "From the Positive to the Regulatory State: Causes and Consequences from Changes in the Modes of Governance," *Journal of Public Policy,* 17 (2) (1997): 139–167.

they wanted to protect positive freedoms, but through market initiatives. Today, the Conservatives of the UK under David Cameron even go as far as to call for a modern and radical Conservatism, which is a contradiction in terms.

Globalization continued a spiral of power away from the state and towards global institutions, with the fall of communism acting as a major force increasing this trend. Globalization has also caused a further change with a push of power down to the local level. This is in full support with the philosophy of liberalism and it shows that the state of the world today can largely be described as a liberal one. Liberal internationalism can seek to harness this global movement for the greater good of society. What is very noticeable in this period is the complete breakdown of the Bretton Woods Institutions in the way they were originally set up. Arising out of these ashes is what has come to be known as the Washington Consensus. The Washington Consensus is essentially aligned very strongly with the notions of neoliberalism and it came about as a reaction to the collapse of the Bretton Woods structure when President Richard M. Nixon pulled out of aligning American currency with gold. This Washington Consensus seeks to apply neoliberalism through the institutions left over from Bretton Woods to alter the domestic structures of developing countries.

All of these major changes were in line with the continual pull from the force of globalization. Kenichi Ohmae goes so far as to say that the nation-state has become 'fiction' in our borderless world. The concept of globalization has come under many different definitions. There is firstly a fundamental difference between talking about globalization on the economic level and talking about it under the broader heading of sociocultural, technological and communicative approaches. At the economic level, "it refers to the reduction and removal of barriers between national borders in order to facilitate the flow of goods, capital, services and labour."[63]

As was shown previously, the basis of modern globalization can be traced back to the Bretton Woods Conference that took

---

63 *Summary of the Annual Review of Developments in Globalization and Regional Integration in the Countries of the ESCWA Region* (United Nations Economic and Social Commission for Western Asia): 1.

place shortly after the Second World War. The fundamental changes brought forth by this system related directly to the increasing liberalization of markets, and with the WTO there was the added increase in international trade. Financial markets have further integrated themselves according to the ease with which they can work together. In the 1970s there was a collapse of their purpose when Nixon pulled away from the gold standard. This led to a restructuring of the purposes of these organizations. The institutions of the World Bank and the International Monetary Fund were initiated. All of these were built to liberalize markets around the world.

Further bilateral and regional trade agreements have been made following this, such as NAFTA — the North American Free Trade Agreement. There was also an increasing need for financial stability leading to the building of the Basel Committee. This is a committee composed of Central Bank governors and seeks to find common standards to be shared by banks across the major economic jurisdictions of the world. The major standards produced are the capital adequacy requirements. These requirements are meant to allow banks to remain stable during times of a crisis as they have a cushion of capital to hold them through the tough times.

Alongside this economic globalization also came a rise in technological and communication changes, as well as a form of cultural globalization. There is another form of globalization that takes a broader view, inclusive of technological and communication changes. This globalization has continued to change and empower the individual in the forms of the family and civil society. It has also brought more power away from the nation state and spurred a greater demand for global governance, even if that hasn't always been met.

The foundation of New Liberalism is still at its core the individual. The individual and the freedom of that individual are the guiding principles to creating a fairer and a more just world. The individual requires a form of liberalism that affects them where they live, work and take part in community activities.

The individual had never before been so empowered as it became under this period when there was a rapid rise in civil society. In fact, it could be argued that the local became global when individuals helped to bring forth a global civil society that filled in the gaps left from a lack of proper global governance. There were also further changes at the local level, including the structure of families.

There has also been a stronger pull down to the individual than ever, in the growth of the civil society. In fact, this individualism has come to replace certain forms of global governance. It can be seen that the state in this modern age relies upon and needs a strong, functioning civil society. There is a growth in public-private partnerships that has not been seen before. We have also seen the civil society go global in this modern era. This growth of global civil society has dramatically altered the game in which people have argued global governance has not come fast enough. They already have large successes as well, including all of the recent human rights bodies and the Ottawa Treaty or the Anti-Personnel Mine Ban Convention, which stopped the production and development of land mines meant to kill individuals. In an age where people are hoping to make a difference, civil society allows them to participate and be engaged in as direct a manner as possible. The number of non-governmental organizations, or NGOs, has skyrocketed, bringing a wider range of issues to the forefront of governance and policy development.

NGOs have been instrumental in bringing forward the key threats to our future, whether it is deficits, climate change or global inequality. Civil society has become the bedrock of a new liberal social contract. The London School of Economics Centre defines Civil Society as "the arena of un-coerced collective action around shared interests, purposes and values."[64] Civil Society has two roles to play in modern society — one is the view that society

---

64 Centre for Civil Society, "What is civil society?" (London School of Economics, 2004). http://www.lse.ac.uk/collections/CCS/what_is_civil_society.htm, retrieved July 12 2010.

needs to keep a check on the state, and the other is the view of associational democracy, whereby it takes part through the state to make a change.[65] One of the most powerful tools that can empower individuals is the internet. The internet can be used as a check on the state, as seen through the work of William Dutton and his writings on the fifth estate.

Liberalism has also influenced the institutions arguably closest to the individual, that of the family and the community. The family has itself become a microcosm of the new social contract. Now husband and wife are treated as equals and the style of relationship has entirely been uplifted. This influence of liberalism has positively benefitted each member of the family through the revolution it has brought forth. This New Liberalism has enabled a family to have more social cohesion in a globalized world than it ever had previously. A liberal family accepts husband and wife as equals in a relationship that focuses on discussion and agreement. These changes are necessary in a world where more women have entered the paid labour force than ever before. There has also been a growth in the responsibility parents are expected to extend to their children.

A good discussion of freedom being extended into the family can be found in the The Third Way: The Renewal of Social Democracy by Anthony Giddens, which shows that the role of the family is changing from a ceremonial role, to the role of people with rights in a familial situation.[66] This is the only way to bring the family into a 21st Century conception. Having a stable family does not rub against individual freedoms — in fact there is no greater creator of freedom through development than having a strong, stable family. This stability can come several different ways through several different measures. Equality of family members is integral to an understanding of families.

---

65 Lucio, B., "Civil Society Meets the State: Towards Associational Democracy," *Socio-Economic Review* (2005). **http://ser.oxfordjournals.org/cgi/reprint/mwj031v1.pdf**, retrieved November 15 2009.

66 Giddens, Anthony, *The Third Way: The Renewal of Social Democracy* (Cambridge: Polity Press, 1998): 89-98.

Liberalism and family go hand-in-hand. The strongest modern families are those based upon liberal values. A family where a husband and wife are considered equals is a liberal idea — as is a marriage or family where freedom from harm is central. A family that says it is right for women to have the choice to work and help provide for a family economically reflects a liberal concept of freedom. If we are talking about free marriages based upon free choice, then we are talking about a liberal marriage.

The community is the closest level of governance to the individual and it is for this simple reason it should be strengthened whenever possible. The more power is devolved to free individuals, the more correct decisions taken. Devolution to the community is needed. These reforms were seen when Prime Minister Tony Blair devolved power to Scotland, Northern Ireland and Wales. They were also seen in Canadian Prime Minister Paul Martin's New Deal for Cities and Communities, in which more power was given to municipalities. These processes of reform must continue. We could also see that municipalities are leading the way in the fight against climate change. The global has become local and the local has become global. These are the actors who have reacted swiftly with regards to climate change and it is only set to continue.

The growth of international organizations has represented a strong shift in the sphere of the social contract. No longer are individuals living merely within the social contract of the state but now find themselves falling under the decision-making powers of far broader and far more plural institutions. The UN needs to be reformed to make it a more democratic and more accountable organization. Liberal democracies have been giving certain powers, rightly, to these higher organizations but in return these institutions have to mirror the interests of the majority of countries. The rise of the United Nations has shown the organization to be a primary source for global governance, and yet it needs to have a continual focus on democratization in order to make it accountable and legitimate. One such proposal is the creation of a United Nations Parliamentary Assembly to bring the institutions of the United Nations closer to the public.

Recently global governance regimes have been extended to include the International Criminal Court. This has been an important addition to the international regime because it ensures we have a safer, more secure world where major war criminals can be put on trial. The principle behind the ICC is it only applies if the states have signed up to the treaty and it only applies as the court of last resort. The purpose of the ICC is to try political leaders of war crimes in a courtroom so as to ensure justice is done. It came into effect in 2002, when it was able to attain the required number of signatories among those nations who ratified the agreement. This is a strong step forward in ensuring a safer world, where criminals of the highest level can be properly tried. The International Court of Justice, or ICJ, is different in the sense it seeks to make judgments based upon cases the member states bring themselves to resolve disputes — it only allows states to bring cases forward.

Less state, more market, stronger individuals and a greater pull of power to the global level. This sums up the market-based social contract. Unfortunately, the global institutions haven't kept pace with the rise of globalization and this is something that will need to be targeted in the future.

ROLE OF THE STATE

During the post-war growth of international organizations there were two forms of social contract, one favouring government and one favouring markets. When positive freedoms were combined with these two forms of social contract, varying roles for the state resulted. The first role for the state was all-encompassing. This was best represented by the welfare states that were instituted by the great liberals Beveridge, US President Franklin Delano Roosevelt and Canadian Prime Ministers Mackenzie King and

Lester Pearson (1897–1972). The second role required smaller government and was pushed by UK Prime Minister Margaret Thatcher and US President Ronald Reagan and continued by UK Prime Minister Tony Blair, US President Bill Clinton and Canadian Prime Minister Jean Chrétien.

The key role of the government under the state-based social contract was seen as laying down the foundations of the welfare state. The very purpose of the welfare state is to ensure everyone in society has the freedom to develop. This is why health care and education were provided, a social safety net was created and pension plans were instituted.

The key characters who implemented the welfare states in their respective countries were of a new kind of leader, one who understood the difference between providing freedoms to people as opposed to controlling the lives of individuals. This requires leaders who value the empowerment of individuals and who see the role of the government as only to open opportunities, not to control the daily life of its citizens.

In the United Kingdom, the welfare state was established by the liberal governments that came slightly before the First World War, with the introduction of the Liberal welfare reforms. The true father of the UK welfare state is the Liberal former Director of the LSE, William Beveridge, who sought to tackle the five giants that hinder freedom: squalor, ignorance, want, idleness and disease.

Within Canada, the focus on positive freedoms was largely extended through the efforts of Mackenzie King and Lester Pearson. It is arguably because of the efforts of these leaders that health care and pension plans exist at the national level. Mackenzie King was a figure that dominated Canadian politics for twenty-one years, longer than any other Prime Minister in the Commonwealth. He had a hand in laying out the basis of the welfare state in Canada with the support of the Progressive Party of Canada. Louis St. Laurent continued with these reforms but it was Lester Pearson who truly carved out the welfare state as it is known in Canada today. He is notable for being the Canadian who introduced health care at a federal level to all

Canadians, with the assistance of Paul Martin Sr., his Minister of Health. Lester Pearson also introduced the Canadian Pension Plan, Canada Student Loans, the forty-hour work week, the minimum wage and a two-week vacation period.

Within the United States of America, it was the New Deal that really served as a framework for American politics for the next fifty years. The New Deal references the acts that were implemented from 1933–1936 to deal with the Great Depression and chart an entirely new form of active government for the United States.

The market-based social contract caused a major change in the role of the state. It was this second social contract where the 21st Century really began. The Thatcher revolution may have called for a smaller role for the state and a greater role for the markets but it is a myth to say she dismantled the welfare state — in fact, the government grew under both Thatcher and Reagan, including the size of their deficits. It would be disingenuous to say they scrapped the major functions of the state, including providing education and health care. It is fair to say privatization and deregulation took place. It was Thatcher who said, "There can be no liberty unless there is economic liberty."[67] There was mass privatization under the Thatcher government, including British Petroleum, British Telecoms and British Steel. The list of privatizations is long and was a major feature of her leadership. Reagan put the concept of freedom and liberty at the heart of his agenda. Reagan once said "Above all, we must realize that no arsenal, or no weapon in the arsenals of the world, is so formidable as the will and moral courage of free men and women. It is a weapon our adversaries in today's world do not have."[68] He further stated, "Freedom is never more than one generation away from extinction. We didn't pass it to our children in the bloodstream. It must be fought for, protected and handed on for them to do the same." John Williamson offered a detailed description of what neoliberalism stands for, stating the Washington Consensus, the original form of neoliberalism,

---

67 Angela, Bonnie; Melville, Frank, "An Interview with Thatcher," *Time Magazine* (May 14 1979): 3.
68 Reagan, Ronald, *First Inaugural Address* (1981).

sought to achieve several objectives, including taking money from subsidies and putting it towards pro-growth and pro-poor services as well as goals like liberalization, privatization and deregulation.

The Chicago school of economics largely supported the economic foundations of neoliberalism with an emphasis on less government intervention and regulation. It attacks Keynesianism as inefficient. Margaret Thatcher stated that her theoretical underpinnings were the work of Friedrich Hayek, especially his *The Constitution of Liberty*. There is no question that Thatcher cut public spending, but in no way did she make it obsolete. In fact, a national health service remained supported by the government throughout her whole term. The neoliberal vision of the role of the state was to be replaced by the politicians of the 'Third Way'. Third Way politicians continued to focus on using markets to fulfill desired outcomes, as well as increasing the amount of money going to the essential services that open up opportunity such as health care and education. This naturally changed under deregulation, the language for which largely came from the Thatcher revolution. These reforms under deregulation continued in the US under Clinton and the Democrats, and in the UK under Blair and the Labour party. Progressive politicians of this time took a while to accept the role of markets and Clinton and Blair really started that shift.

Clinton was an early advocate of mainstream politics in his Democratic Party, joining and eventually becoming president of the Democratic Leadership Council. When running for President, there was a strong focus on welfare reform and a smaller role for the government. In the United Kingdom, we saw Blair adopt similar concepts, as well as relying upon the writings of Anthony Giddens and his concept of the Third Way. Blair spoke about modernizing the Labour Party and, as a result, was able to extend his vote to the south of England, which for a long time had eluded the grasp of any Labour candidate.

The Third Way also played a major role within Australian politics. The Labor Party under Prime Minister Bob Hawke and Prime Minister Paul Keating really pushed for adoption of fiscally responsible economic measures. This included floating the Australian dollar in 1983, privatization of Qantas among other assets and deregulation. Kevin Rudd of the Labor Party continued in this vein of centre-left politics oriented around fiscal responsibility.

Under Jean Chrétien and Paul Martin, we saw Canada go from a forty-two billion dollar deficit to a surplus. Furthermore, thirty-six billion dollars were paid down on the country's debt. It cut its fiscal deficit and debt, becoming one of the strongest economies in the G8, while at the same time, continuing to maintain universal health care and education systems.

Until the financial crisis of 2008, the general state of the relationship between the state and markets swung drastically in the direction of markets. Leaders of all political stripes were consistently calling for a smaller state. In actuality, the state still maintained its essential functions of protecting positive as well as negative freedoms.

The major theories that have been implemented by governments generally fall under neoliberalism, the Third Way and compassionate conservatism. In practice the markets are still mixed markets wherever you go. There is no such thing as a purely free market. There has been a growth in civil society, especially at the international level, something not seen at any time previous and increasing signs of globalization. The state itself was pared down, with a greater devolution of powers to regional governments, as well as a growth in the number of international bodies.

The Third Way is intrinsically different from "capitalism with its unswerving belief in the merits of the free market and democratic socialism with its demand management and obsession with the state. The Third Way is in favour of growth, entrepreneurship, enterprise and wealth creation but it is also in favour of greater social justice and it sees the state playing a major role in bringing this about. So in the words of Giddens, the Third Way rejects top-down socialism as it rejects traditional neoliberalism."[69] This new movement was therefore founded upon

---

69 "What is the Third Way?" BBC News (September 27 1999). http://news.bbc.co.uk/2/hi/458626.stm, retrieved February 25 2010..

a new philosophy which could transcend the debates of traditional socialism and neoliberalism and find a new ground. This Third Way philosophy adopted the market as a component of the model.

In the Third Way, the individual was actually placed at the centre of this new structure. The security of the individual produced a focus on crime. The democratization of the family was the empowerment of individuals within it. These changes adapted social democracy to revolve around the use of the state to ensure both positive and negative freedoms for the individual, thus demonstrating the Third Way as a form of social liberalism. Just as conservatism went through the phase of neoliberalism to adapt its structures to the current understanding that positive and negative freedoms of the individual are desirable, so too did the Third Way adapt social democracy to accepting that positive and negative freedoms revolving around the individual are desirable.

In fact, Giddens made the argument that conservatism failed after Thatcher because on the one hand it argued market fundamentalism, the idea that the individual should be free, and on the other that traditional notions of family should be forced upon individuals. It was the philosophy of the Third Way which in fact adapted the traditional units of family around the individual in the modern time. The idea of devolution itself is centred around the idea of bringing society closer to the individual.

At this point in time, conservatives came in with a full admission that positive freedoms were an integral function of society but the disagreement remained as to how much should be controlled by the market and how much by the state. This is a fair debate but one that fully agrees on the core principle that positive and negative freedoms are essential for the individual in continuation of the social liberal tradition. In fact, this conservatism also adopted the liberal internationalist theory that democracy and human rights should be spread as a concept throughout the world.

Compassionate conservatism revolves around the idea positive freedoms can best be met using market mechanisms. Michael Gerson, speech writer for George W. Bush, said, "Compassionate conservatism is the theory the government should encourage the effective provision of social services without providing the service itself."[70]

It is crucially important to understand that neoconservatism has admitted positive freedoms in society do exist and they need to be protected. What is at variance is how this should be best managed. This is a large thing for a conservative to admit because the traditional conservative philosophy has been that there was no such concept as positive freedoms. At this point in history, it is seen that liberalism has been adopted by all sides, that positive and negative freedoms exist and the only debate that goes on is how to best provide these freedoms. None of these theories can tackle the problems that currently face our society. We need to adapt our knowledge of politics to deal with reality.

FROM SOCIAL TO NEW LIBERALISM

Delving through all of the theories governments have argued to be their guiding purpose, it becomes evident that the freedom and development of the individual has been at the centre of it all. The only debates major parties focus on are how best to bring about positive freedoms with the balance tipping towards either the government or the markets.

This really demonstrates the power of social liberalism in the world and shows the force with which the ideas actually produce the most positive benefits. At the end of the 20th Century, it has been declared liberalism is the end of history,[71] in the sense that this would be the political system to remain in place for the rest of history.

This system does need to change and adapt, so there is still more work to be done. With all the success social liberalism has provided, it cannot tackle the current challenges of our time.

70 Riley, Naomi Schaefer, "Mr. Compassionate Conservatism," *The Wall Street Journal* (October 21 2006): 1.

71 Fukayama, Francis, *The End of History and the Last Man* (Free Press, 1992).

Liberalism is most powerful when it can open up freedom for the most individuals. The reason the challenges we face today are so different is because they do not impact upon the freedoms of people living today, rather they impact on the freedoms of people living tomorrow.

The world is arguably on the brink of a shift to a new liberalism, one based upon protecting the freedom of all people, born now and in the future. It is also born out of the concept of a new social contract taking shape in the aftermath of the financial crisis. The role of the state therefore must be to focus on increasing freedoms within and outside of itself based on these conditions.

The concept of freedom within the state focuses on protecting essential services: implementing policies supporting multiculturalism, making government more accountable and transparent, investing in science and technology and upholding the rule of law. Freedoms external to the state involve dealing with some of the greatest threats of our time — dealing with genocide, terrorism, nuclear disarmament and disease.

Just as classical liberalism was based upon negative freedoms and social liberalism on positive freedoms, now New Liberalism is based around the concept of timeless freedoms. The contours of this new foundational concept of freedom need to be looked at before turning to the shape of the New Social Contract. There has also been a significant shift in the New Social Contract — largely caused by the financial crisis — which has reignited a discussion as to whether markets really are infallible or not. This has increased the role of the state for the near future. It is important government does not remain large merely to hoard powers. It has a duty to use its functions wisely and it needs to do so in a fiscally responsible manner that will not burden future generations with large amounts of debt. It also has to ensure that the correct regulations are in place so future generations won't suffer from a crisis this size.

3

TIMELESS FREEDOM

At the very heart of New Liberalism is a new foundational concept of freedom. Timeless freedom is inherently about ensuring the freedoms of future generations are secured through proactive action taken today. The idea of timeless freedom is needed in order to set out a framework through which liberalism can tackle the great challenges facing humanity. Essentially, the environmental crisis, the financial crisis and the inequality crisis have all exposed cracks in the structure of social liberalism that have been in place from the beginning. These cracks are based upon the short-term view provided by social liberalism and a lack of sustainable planning. The concept of timeless freedom bases itself on the extension of positive and negative freedoms to future generations, therefore adding a new dimension to liberalism. This concept is directly tied to the third generation of human rights and specifically intergenerational equity and sustainability.

This new concept of timeless freedom allows liberalism to be used as a force for good and a force for extending freedoms to future generations. In a period of time when we are freer than ever before, we have also bound ourselves with our own chains. We are not free while these problems linger and are set to fundamentally affect the future of humanity. We are facing threats never seen before in history. Man-made climate change has the potential to wipe out whole communities with rising sea levels and changes to ecosystems. The recent financial crisis showed human nature is such that greed can stop the free market from working in the public interest.

This crisis also led to states piling on massive debt. The debt crisis in Greece is a further sign that not helping future generations can actually hinder people living today. While Greece had fiscal problems previous to the crisis, the recession brought this issue to the forefront and shows how a large debt can negatively impact future generations. The growing gap between rich and poor with a shrinking middle class in-between only further hinders future generations. Liberalism is meant to stand for freedom and yet there is no framework in place to support the freedoms of future generations.

It is important to first understand what timeless freedom is *not*. Timeless freedom is not based around the view that all incidents of the future can be predicted. It however does refocus the state on mitigating risk. It is a framework to provide a proper viewpoint to extend freedoms not only to people today, but to extend freedoms to peoples of tomorrow as well. Real challenges are going to take place. This does not seek to set the priorities for a government, as these are debates that need to be based within each country.

It is not possible to predict the future but it is possible to foresee the consequences of actions taken today, as seen in discussions on the risk society. A fundamental component of this timeless freedom is the concept of the risk society, whereby the state should have the function of protecting against future risks to our freedoms. The risk society is the reason regulation is needed. Risks yet unknown form the other component of the two-fold construction of timeless freedom, alongside the idea that it falls under the role of government to protect against known problems such as fiscal responsibility and climate change.

Anthony Giddens defines the risk society as "a society increasingly preoccupied with the future (and also with safety), which generates the notion of risk".[72] Timeless freedoms fully revolve around the notion of risk through risk prevention and mitigation. The concept defined as manufactured risk has special importance within the idea of timeless freedom. This risk arguably changes how we interact with the world, which has been termed reflexive modernization. The risks we create can be understood by our science and technology, which in turn changes how we react to the risks, leading to concepts such as sustainability, explored later. We are living in a world today where our science can reasonably predict at least some of the risks of the future. These risks are calculable and so serve as known threats to our freedom. These threats require focus if we are to protect the freedoms of the future.

The framework of timeless freedoms is grounded in reality. It is about the necessity of adapting real politics to solving critical problems. These problems are real — they are happening and we have the ability to do something about it. Our response can help us in the short term, as well as ensure our long-term freedoms.

Just as social liberalism is composed of both positive and negative freedom, so too is New Liberalism composed of positive freedom and negative freedom, but extended to people living in the future as well as today. This means the role of the state under New Liberalism will still be to press for these freedoms,while also pursuing the timeless freedoms that are to be discussed. While case studies will deal with climate change, fiscal responsibility and inequality, this is by no means the full extent of timeless freedoms, simply the most pressing issues.

Timeless freedoms have a foundation in the conception of third-generation human rights. Just as negative freedoms were composed of negative rights and negative responsibilities and positive freedoms were composed of second-generation positive rights and responsibilities, so too does timeless freedom have a basis in the third generation of human rights and the responsibilities attached to them. The discussion of human rights lends itself well to this concept of timeless liberty, for human rights are meant to

---

72 Giddens, Anthony, *Runaway World: How Globalization is Reshaping Our Lives* (Routledge, 2000): 3.

apply to all humans at all times. This concept of universalism can be seen in a framework in which rights are owed to individuals who aren't even born yet.

The idea of 'inalienable rights' has the three generations of rights as a precursor to its position in New Liberalism. As has been shown, the first generation deals with negative rights, the second with positive rights and the third with numerous rights including those of intergenerational mobility and sustainability. What is fundamental to freedom is the idea that it is not only rights but also responsibilities that are endowed. The very reason we have rights is they are accepted as inalienable and guaranteed by the society we are living in. We have responsibilities to that society to protect those very rights, leading all the way back to the harm principle of John Stuart Mill. It must be made very clear that third-generation rights are not fully equivalent to timeless freedoms. Though also composed of collective rights and environmental causes, timeless freedoms are about the freedom of the individual. As such, they touch upon intergenerational equity and sustainability — both fundamental components of timeless freedoms. For the idea of liberalism to actually function at all, a concept of freedom has to be timeless.

There are also strong claims to these timeless freedoms being based in the concept of intergenerational equity. Timeless freedom is directly connected to the concept of intergenerational justice — just as former generations have passed on this world and these freedoms to us, we likewise have the responsibility to pass on this just and free world to the next generation, as well as supporting those who gave us this freedom by keeping the promise of dignity, with pension plans for example. Exercising these responsibilities demonstrates the intergenerational contract and intergenerational equity.

Sustainability and sustainable development is directly linked to the concept the planet needs to be looked after in order for humans to survive. The Brundtland Commission of the United Nations on March 20, 1987 said "sustainable development is development that meets the needs of the present without compromising the ability of future generations to meet their own needs."[73] The 2005 World Summit declared the three pillars of sustainability to be social, economic and environmental concerns. The growth of this concept of sustainability really arose with the consciousness of the impact of the industrial revolution on the environment. Several books triggered an understanding that there are potentially detrimental effects from certain activities. This spurred a shift towards sustainable living, with a rise in recycling and other environmentally friendly activities. We are now aware that we are harming our atmosphere through global warming and our oceans with pollution, and so actively make efforts to mitigate if not reverse our impact. The impact of humans is generally expressed in the formula where the population is multiplied by their affluence and their technology.

The concept of timeless freedoms truly pushes our current institutions to the extent of their abilities. Democracies, markets and individuals are all predisposed to thinking in the short term yet it is these long-term challenges that truly threaten our freedom. One positive sign from all this is when people internalize future threats, the short-termism is adapted to revolve around long-term challenges. We already see increasing action taken on climate change by politicians and concerned citizens around the world. One example to be explored further is the cap-and-trade system. Here we have governments and markets working together to use the institutions we have to correct these long-term difficulties.

Timeless freedom can claim some relationship to green liberalism, the idea we are people of nature and therefore our freedoms are threatened if we destroy the environment in which we live. The concept of timeless freedom disagrees with the proposition nature has any rights itself, as it is the individual's

---

73 World Commission on Environment and Development, *Our Common Future* (Oxford: Oxford University Press, 1987): 1.

freedom that forms its basis. While timeless freedom does not disagree with this view of the importance of preserving the integrity of nature, it is the freedom of the individual that is of direct concern. Climate change in particular is seen as an perfect illustration of the concept of timeless freedoms because it threatens humanity itself, not just nature.

The very idea of social mobility is based upon the concept someone should be able to rise up in the future. Providing education is by definition trying to open up freedoms for future generations. These concepts of intergenerational equity and sustainability are well-documented but it is important to frame them in the context of freedom as it relates to us and not merely to some notion of fairness and equity.

Intergenerational equity is a form of thinking based in social justice that embraces the idea that future generations deserve the same rights we currently have. There is a major difference between a mere desire for social justice and preserving the beauty of the planet. This concept of intergenerational equity has been defined as when "needs of the present [are met] without compromising the ability of future generations to meet their own needs."[74]

Just as we had a responsibility not to harm others and a mutual responsibility to our community, so too do we have a responsibility to our children and the future generations that will occupy our cities, provinces, country and planet. We are able to have freedom but we also have a responsibility to protect and preserve freedom for future generations. These are our mutual obligations to all members of society, tying back together with the common good and the idea we rise and fall together.

This concept of timeless freedom serves as the foundation of New Liberalism. A country that adopts this approach to politics will have a society that will be stronger for future generations but can in fact be a net plus for those living today as well. It only takes looking to Greece to see the problems debt can have on those living today. The three greatest threats to future freedoms will be

---

74 United Nations, "Report of the World Commission on Environment and Development," General Assembly Resolution 42/187 (December 11 1987): 1.

explored and how these can be turned into benefits for today and the future.

Timeless freedom is based upon the concept of rights, responsibilities, intergenerational equity, sustainability and the risk society. This reframes the issues to their core element, a threat to the freedom of human society. Should nothing be done, then it isn't because we weren't generous enough, it is because we didn't realize this is a direct threat to our humanity. Timeless freedom is ultimately in place to stop the dynamic Hobhouse describes with "The evil that is done in the present day may only bear fruit when the generation that has done it has passed away."[75]

CLIMATE CHANGE AND ENERGY SECURITY

The most fundamental threat currently facing humanity is the threat of man-made global warming. This is directly connected to the threat of peak oil and the concepts of energy security and the geopolitics of energy. These two issues are both threats to our well-being and are important to address because we can actually do something about them. We have the ability to create the new technologies to deal with these issues and as long as we work hard in creating more new green jobs, implementing cap-and-trade and applying the latest technologies, we will be that much closer to ensuring the freedom of humanity. However, technological fixes are not the end of the equation, as we need to change the behaviours of individuals and communities to institute long-term reform, and this includes a change in environmental consciousness. It is important to assess what action the state can take, before looking at the direction of global and local agreements that can bolster the action of states.

The threat of climate change is fundamentally different from other environmental topics, as climate change is a direct threat to individuals and it is for this reason it fits within the framework of liberalism. This also applies to the concept of energy security.

---

75 Hobhouse, L.T., *Liberalism* (Middlesex: The Echo Library, 2009 [1911]): 29.

As Giddens points out, the planet will still be here whether we are on it or not.[76] Climate change offers threats to human freedoms such as rising sea levels, mass migrations and greater natural disasters.

At the heart of the low-carbon economy is the idea greenhouse gas emissions will be reduced. The reason this must be a priority in our society is because science has shown a rise in greenhouse gases will cause the climate to change, leading to adverse effects for the planet. Several technologies are already in place to start tackling this challenge and there are further technological advances yet to be introduced. Examples of current renewable energies include nuclear, solar and wind power. The International Energy Agency defines renewable energy as being "derived from natural processes that are replenished constantly. In its various forms, it derives directly from the sun or from heat generated deep within the earth. Included in the definition is electricity and heat generated from solar, wind, ocean, hydro power, biomass, geothermal resources, and biofuels and hydrogen derived from renewable resources." [77] Furthermore, there are advances in new technologies all the time, including the concept of carbon capture and storage. There are also market changes that can be put in place, such as cap-and-trade. A cap-and-trade system seeks to use economic incentives to reduce carbon emissions and is a market-based approach.

This state action has been given a direction at the global level through the United Nations Framework Convention on Climate Change, which came about from the Rio de Janeiro meeting of world leaders in 1992. There is a yearly conference to discuss this treaty and to propose global agreements to tackle climate change. The most well-known agreement to date is the Kyoto Protocol.

Kyoto is known because it gave developed countries, described as Annex I countries, hard targets to be compliant. Hard targets are specific levels of reductions in emissions that a country needs to meet in order to comply with the agreement.

---

76 Giddens, Anthony, *The Politics of Climate Change* (Cambridge: Polity Press, 2009): 56.
77 Janssen, Rodney and the Renewable Energy Working Party, *Renewable Energy . . . into the Mainstream* (International Energy Agency, 2003): 9.

One key aspect attached to it was that Annex I countries could use flexible mechanisms to reduce their emissions, which means that a country can either purchase the emission reductions from other countries or they can build clean industries in other countries through either joint implementation or the Clean Development Mechanism (CDM). Joint implementation is the idea Annex I countries can build in other Annex I countries. Originally the climate-change debate brought about large divisions between developed and developing countries. There were several reasons for this rift, namely that developed countries pollute far more per capita than any developing country, that this has been going on for a long time in developed countries with all historical emissions included, the fact developed countries have already hit economic maturity where undeveloped countries have not (economic maturity is when GDP growth does not come with a growth in energy consumption), there is a right-to-development argument for developing countries and the argument that dealing with climate change should focus on ideas that empower developing countries such as technology transfer.

In the beginning, environmentalists originally argued mitigation should be the sole concern for dealing with global emissions. This turned Kyoto into a treaty on target reductions. Since then, there has been growing acceptance that adaptation also needs to be considered. Where mitigation seeks to slow the effects of climate change, adaptation seeks to prepare society for the changes that will happen due to climate change. Examples include building defences against rising sea levels and enhancing the adaptive capacity of those most vulnerable to the effects of global warming. Adaptive capacity is improved through increased education and reduced poverty.

Another key issue that has entered the negotiations of climate change is the issue of forests, which add a complex layer to the debate. Twenty percent of greenhouse gases come from deforestation. The REDD program has been instituted to counteract this problem. REDD stands for Reducing Emissions from Deforestation and forest Degradation and it aims to combat this grave problem.

The most recent conference held in Cancun reached an agreement to keep the rise in global temperature below 2° Celsius above pre-industrial levels, set up a Green Climate Fund to aid poorer countries and set up a Green Climate Fund to aid poorer countries and included a system of funding to avoid deforestation. It further includes agreements on moving forward on adaptation and technology transfer, as well as codifying the emission-reduction targets set by the Copenhagen Accord signed the year previously. The Accord said "deep cuts in global emissions are required according to science . . . with a view to reduce global emissions so as to hold the increase in global temperature below 2 degrees Celsius and take action to meet this objective consistent with science".[78] U.S. President Obama said, "Science dictates even more needs to be done."[79] It is also debatable as to whether this target is within reach under this framework.

Ultimately, the Copenhagen Accord that came before the Cancun Agreement was unsuccessful in large measure. This agreement did not set national targets, was not legally binding and was not global. It could really have been called the Five-Nation Deal, though it was better than nothing. Even though not official, it still had been taken note of by the United Nations Framework Convention on Climate Change (UNFCCC); included discussions on mitigation, adaptation, technology transfer and forests; and it included the signatures of the United States of America, China, Brazil, South Africa and India.

While agreement at the global level has proven difficult, action at the grassroots level has really spurred all of the major action currently taken on tackling man-made climate change. It has been a bottom-up approach. The cities have agreed even where no global agreement has been found. The technologies that will do the most to change will come from the imagination of people who come up with the ideas on their own. This includes the renewable

---

78 UNFCCC (2009) Copenhagen Accord. Draft decision -/CP.15, FCCC/CP/2009/L.7 [*electronic version*] unfccc.int/resource/docs/2009/cop15/eng/l07.pdf, retrieved December 25 2010.
79 Obama, Barack, *Copenhagen Conference* (2009).

energy businesses. The public opinion dealing with climate change will also ensure that world leaders stay focused on tackling this grave crisis. Climate change was brought into public consciousness through the efforts of NGOs. The actual power of NGOs has been put forth most succinctly by Keck and Sikkink, who state they allow "ecological values to be placed above narrow definitions of national interest."[80] They also "help establish a common language and sometimes, common world views".[81] It is at this local level the most has been done to bring the debate forward, and it is at this level that even more action needs to be taken.

Tied to this concept of climate change has been the concept of peak oil. This is the concept that at a certain point, the extraction of petroleum will reach its maximum point, at which point production will continue to fall and decline until it eventually depletes. M. King Hubbert (1903–1989) first created the models that predicted peak oil would be reached in America between 1965 and 1970, known as the Hubbert Peak Theory. Peak oil has the potential to seriously disrupt the future of our planet. Giddens argues that the politics of energy security and climate change go hand-in-hand. Taking action on creating renewable energy will not only help the planet, it will also help prevent war. If nothing is done about shrinking oil reserves, a power struggle could break out leading to violence. Green jobs are essential to the economy of tomorrow and a low-carbon economy. Jobs in the energy field are powerful because they are jobs that cannot be shipped overseas, a powerful incentive in an age when globalization reigns.

Self-interest in climate change is found through the creation of jobs and through the complete betterment of society. At the heart of New Liberalism is the idea that protecting future freedoms will also protect current freedoms. Looking out for the people of today necessarily goes hand-in-hand with looking after the people

---

80 Keck, Margaret E.; Sikkink, Kathryn, *Activists Beyond Borders: Advocacy Networks in International Politics* (Ithaca and London: Cornell University Press, 1998): 215.

81 Princen, T., Finger, M., Manno, J.P., "Translational linkages," in *Environmental NGOs in World Politics: Linking the Local and the Global,* ed. T. Princen and M. Finger (Routledge, London, 1994): 218-36.

of tomorrow — through creative initiatives the people of today will actually be better off. The largest economic engines of today depend heavily on oil, presenting challenges on several fronts. In the areas of the environment and energy security, a whole marketplace of green jobs and energy exists which will directly improve the economy of those countries that are forward-looking and real innovators in protecting the freedoms of tomorrow.

Action *now* on climate change is truly at the heart of this idea of New Liberalism. We have a responsibility to uphold the freedoms of future generations which would be infringed on by climate change — not just out of intergenerational equity but because of a duty to ensure the freedom of humanity itself. Should we fulfill our obligations, we will also have created more jobs, a stronger economic base that cannot be exported overseas and, ultimately, the economy of the future — one that will not be held back by security concerns over energy.

FISCAL RESPONSIBILITY

At the heart of fiscal responsibility, two distinct and important areas need to be examined — the state budget and the regulatory system in place to assess potential crises for future generations. The issue of debt is connected with the idea future generations will have to pay more taxes to keep up with the interest the country will need to pay on loans. The issue of debt is further correlated with the amount of private investment a country receives. Where debt is high, there is a general trend towards less private investment in the economy. Without fiscal discipline, future generations will suffer. The financial crisis demonstrated that lack of proper regulatory structures will cause future generations to suffer. It is truly important to understand that balanced budgets and proper regulatory frameworks actually benefit short-term interests as well as long-term interests. In the short term, greater investment goes to those countries that have a proven record of running balanced budgets.

There are two key features to fiscal responsibility and stability, responsible budgets and appropriate regulations in place. Budgets run improperly over the long term can have horrible effects for future generations but, just as importantly, can hurt the present as well. In *The Public Debt: A Burden on Future Generations?*, William G. Bowen, Richard G. Davis and David H. Kopf argued it is in fact possible to pass on the burden to the next generation.[82] Fiscal irresponsibility was actually one of the major causes for the collapse of the Weimar Republic in Germany and, as a result, one of the major reasons for the rise of Adolf Hitler. One needs only look at present-day Greece to see the problems created when action is not taken to address growing national debts — when generation after generation grows the size of debt, it causes pain to current and future generations.

A person will not be born free if they are burdened by the debt of their forefathers. Jean Chrétien and Paul Martin in Canada understood this concept when they were able to present balanced budgets during their tenures. When Chrétien was elected Prime Minister of Canada in 1993, he focused his government on reducing the federal debt and deficit with the support of Martin, then Minister of Finance. Within their time in office, they eliminated 42 billion dollars of deficit, paying back 36 billion dollars on their debt as well, which was followed by an economic recovery in their country.

The current fiscal crisis naturally led to the majority of developed countries providing stimulus plans to boost their economy. This kind of reparative approach may be necessary in the short term but in the long term, fiscal discipline needs to be reintegrated — without such action being taken, future generations will be forced to shoulder the burden. A stimulus plan is essential for restoring economic health in the short term but when stability returns to the system, it will need to be refocused on cutting the debt and deficit to restore the budget to fiscal health. The words of President Eisenhower (1890–1969) show an even stronger position:

---

82 Bowen, William G.; Davis, Richard G.; Kopf, David H., "The Public Debt: A Burden on Future Generations?" *The American Economic Review* Vol. 50, No. 4 (1960): 701-706.

"Personally, I do not feel any amount can be properly called a surplus as long as the nation is in debt. I prefer to think of such an item as a reduction on our children's inherited mortgage".[83] Caring about future generations through balanced budgets actually improves the lives of those of us living today. It means less interest to pay every year and greater private investment in a country — on top of the confidence a country attains from knowing it is in a financially secure position.

At the heart of the financial crisis was excessive risk-taking. Sub-prime mortgages were given out at excessive levels. These mortgages were themselves securitized and diversified so credit rating agencies marked them as low-risk, when in reality a drop in the housing market was all that was needed for the defaults to start pouring in and credit to stop flowing. Once the credit stopped flowing, banks started to collapse. With consumer banks collapsing, the contagion spread to investment banks. The thing about investment banks is that it wasn't realized how integral they had become to the entire banking sector and how their failure could cause systemic risk. This has led to post-crisis calls to start regulating them.

The actions taken by the Obama administration in the United States, on top of a stimulus plan, were to create a Consumer Protection Agency, insist on greater capital requirements, regulation of derivatives, demand greater accountability and transparency of financial products and restore market integrity. There was also a broad agreement to enhance international coordination and cooperation of regulatory agencies, notably including much talk on reforming the system of compensation to address longer-term thinking.

Fundamentally in line with the concept of New Liberalism, Joseph Stiglitz strongly makes the point that executive compensation should be more related to long-term performance,[84] He also stated they should re-instate Glass-Steagal, the US

---

83 Eisenhower, D., *State of the Union Message* (1960).
84 "Stiglitz Recommendations," *CNN* (September 17 2008). http://www.cnn.com/2008/POLITICS/09/17/stiglitz.crisis/index.html, retrieved June 20 2010.

Banking Act of 1933, which would ensure that investment banks could not take the same risks as commercial banks. Paul Krugman states regulation should be in place for banks as well as institutions that "act like banks".[85] Raghuram Rajan suggests, in line with New Liberalism, that financial institutions should maintain 'contingent capital', which means paying the government during boom periods, with the government reimbursing banks in downturns.[86] The Volcker Rule, a proposal by former US Federal Reserve chairman Paul Volcker, aimed to restrict banks from speculating in ways that wouldn't benefit consumers.[87] The housing bubble should have been popped a lot sooner than it was. It was irresponsible not to do so — bubbles need to be popped before they gain enough size and position to collapse a system.[88]

When push came to shove, politicians of all stripes adopted Keynesian thinking, whether Conservative or Liberal, Republican or Democratic. Regulation must be in place to limit the chance of a major financial collapse from taking place again. Fiscal irresponsibility threatens our children and our children's children. The state has two fundamental roles — one is to ensure responsible budgets are put forth and the other is to establish proper regulations. Ultimately, the state needs to start thinking long-term and put in place a financially sustainable system of governance.

INEQUALITY

The very nature of inequality and poverty is not such that it just provides a threat to freedoms of today but, further, it threatens

---

85 Krugman, Paul, *The Return of Depression Economics and the Crisis of 2008* (W.W. Norton Company Limited, 2009): 189-190.

86 "The Economist-Rajan-Cycle Proof Regulation," *The Economist* (April 8 2009). http://www.economist.com/finance/displaystory.cfm?story_id=13446173, retrieved July 21 2010.

87 Uchitelle, Louis, "Glass-Steagall vs. the Volcker Rule", *The New York Times* (January 22 2010). http://economix.blogs.nytimes.com/2010/01/22/glass-steagall-vs-the-volcker-rule/, retrieved February 15 2010.

88 Roubini, Nouriel, *Why Central Banks Should Burst Bubbles* (Stern School of Business, NYU, 2005).

the freedoms of future generations. It is very straightforward to say that people with less money do not have as much freedom and opportunity in this world. They statistically have shorter lifespans, a greater likelihood of depression and suicide and are more likely to contract diseases. This inequality in future generations must be addressed, not merely the current population suffering from inequality. This discussion applies both within a country and externally.

Several potential sources bring about these institutionalized inequalities. Some are based on limitations in educational opportunities, while others relate to race, gender, job opportunities, a person's individual talents and the freedom of choice to do as much or as little as one likes in relation to their work ethic. Social liberalism by its very nature stands up for increasing educational opportunities as a form of freedom to develop. It also stands for equality regardless of race or gender. The general approach to solving these problems has been to invest in public education, progressive taxation and minimum wage laws. The welfare state has helped to give health care to all individuals in need. The studies show that economic liberalism also reduces global economic inequality around the world.

This concept of inequality affecting future generations is best correlated with intergenerational mobility. Future generations should not have fewer opportunities merely because of the family they were born into. Our society cannot say it has free citizens if birth controls the rest of one's life. If this is truly the case, than we have not progressed from the hereditary right liberalism fought against from the very beginning. We should not be consigned to the position we were born into if we have the drive to do more.

The effect inequalities have on future generations and also intergenerational mobility need to be focused on. At the core of this argument is the poverty trap — poverty in fact inhibits three generations of a single family merely because of the presence of poverty in the first generation. This means that even the grandchildren of a person under the poverty line will generally also find themselves below the poverty line. The poverty cycle is a "set of factors or events by which poverty, once started, is likely to continue unless there is outside intervention".[89] This leads to generational poverty. With a shrinking middle class and a growing gap between rich and poor, this is an issue that is rising in urgency.

Global poverty acting as a barrier to future generations revolves around equality of opportunities. Poverty is the greatest inhibitor to the creation of opportunity in the world. At the extreme end of intergenerational mobility are those children born to parents in poverty. Where a child has the natural intelligence to be a doctor or a lawyer, they are often unable to achieve their potential solely due to where they were born and how much their parents earn and, as a result, are resigned to child poverty. "Children living in poverty are those who experience deprivation of the material, spiritual and emotional resources needed to survive, develop and thrive, leaving them unable to enjoy their rights, achieve full potential or participate as full and equal members of society."[90]

Where poverty causes opportunities to be lost in this world, those opportunities are not only a loss to the individual in question — it is a loss to all of us. Poverty means one cannot afford essential human necessities such as food, health care, education, housing, clothing and water. Owing to necessity, education would likely be the first to be sacrificed, with health care following close behind — notably, both of these impact the next generation's potential to earn money. Extending negative and positive freedoms necessarily means addressing the issues at the core of poverty. Protecting property rights like land and providing financial services to the poor will increase economic opportunity while government-subsidized health care and education will give them the foundation and tools necessary to be more productive. A child born with inadequate ability to attain health care means they are already at a disadvantage trying to learn at school (or even to attend) or to

---

89 "Cycle of Poverty," *The Unabridged Hutchinson Encyclopedia* (Research Machines, 2009).

90 UNICEF *State of the World's Children 2005: Childhood Under Threat* (UNICEF, 2005): 18.

work in later life. Children are at a higher risk of achieving lower grades when they come from a low-income background.[91]

It seems as if poverty is the ultimate lack of freedom. Its causes are directly linked to a lack of freedom for citizens in both a positive and negative sense — they lack democratic government, education, crime prevention and free markets. Increasing democracy, increasing education, fighting crime and opening up markets have not eliminated poverty but have greatly reduced the amount of absolute poverty globally.

Intergenerational mobility is a key plank of timeless freedoms. Future generations should have the freedom to develop just as we have today. This means we must tackle the root causes of poverty both within the state and globally, with a specific focus on children born into poverty. Addressing inequalities in society will ensure we don't return to a system where your birth dictates the rest of your life. Liberalism has always fought against this dynamic and will continue to do so. Just as progressive taxation enabled developed countries to educate an entire workforce, so too would a global reduction in inequalities enable greater freedom and a more just world to take shape.

Two specific initiatives targeted at tackling poverty are tax cuts for middle and lower-income earners and childcare/early education. Tax cuts are necessary in order to help those poorest afford what is most necessary. Childcare is necessary to allow parents to work while ensuring their children are safe and secure. Early education allows children to gain an education to help break the poverty trap. Furthermore, the "State of the World's Children" report by UNICEF "found the greater the proportion of GDP devoted to family allowances, disability and sickness benefits, formal daycare provisions, Employment Insurance and other forms of social assistance, the lower the risk of growing up in poverty."[92]

---

91 Gutman, Leslie Morrison; Sameroff, Arnold J.; Cole, Robert, "Academic Growth Curve Trajectories from 1st Grade to 12th Grade: Effects of Multiple Social Risk Factors and Preschool Child Factors," in *Developmental Psychology* Vol. 39, No. 4 (Jul 2003): 777-790.

92 Albanese, Patrizia, *Child Poverty in Canada* (Oxford University Press Canada, 2009): 180.

The threat to future generations of being stuck in the poverty cycle and not being able to take advantage of opportunities afforded to others is a return to what liberalism stood against, a hereditary system where birth decides your life.

4

New Social Contract

The financial crisis of 2008 created the need for a new social contract and a new negotiation of powers between the state and the market. A fundamental component relating to the role of the state is the amount of power its citizens consent to allow it. This consent changes the horizontal relations between the state and markets and it changes the vertical relations between individuals, the state and the global infrastructure. A large feature of this social contract is also the primary function of the state as well. Where a night watchman state was traditionally sought, an evolution into the welfare state and then the regulatory state took place. The markets themselves have changed from laissez-faire economics, to Keynesian, to neoclassical, to neo-Keynesian. At the local level, the individual has become more and more empowered in this fast-changing and ever-uncertain reality we currently live in. With the rise of globalization combined with liberal internationalism, we have seen a continual growth of international bodies, but this growth has not come as fast as the interconnectedness of the financial markets. This is largely why the effects of the global financial crisis were felt so widely.

It is important to look at the root causes of what creates these large shifts in societal consent for the size of the state. The primary precipitant of change seems to be crisis. The primary causes for the change from the classical social contract to the state-based social contract were two world wars and the Great Depression. The cause for the change from the state-based social contract to the market-based social contract was the recession of the 1970s. Today, change stems from the global financial crisis, which has served as the catalyst for the current social contract we now live in with a greater call for state intervention, more questioning of the role of the markets and an impetus to reform the financial system while ensuring that individuals are still able to have the basic qualities of life.

The impact of crisis as a precipitant for change is mitigated by an understanding that both states and markets have their limits. There are several arguments often made against state competence. Regulatory capture is the concept that industries eventually take control of the rule-making bodies and produce outcomes which serve their own best interests. This is based upon politicians being as self-interested as every other human. There is also the criticism of the state having a large inefficient bureaucracy.

The financial crisis shows the dangers in an unstable and under-regulated free market as well, primarily that it is prone to crisis, which often leads to major changes taking place, in turn reducing the stability of the society. There are also market failure problems such as information deficits, monopolies, anti-competitive behaviour and externalities such as damage to the environment, among others. The whole purpose of regulation is to counteract these types of market failures. Acting together, the limits of the state and the interconnectedness of states show a third weakness and reason for change.

The state also becomes smarter as time goes on. Where it would previously regulate everything itself, it is now able to incorporate businesses and NGOs in the process of regulating. This cedes greater decision-making power to institutions outside of the state, allowing for a broader regulatory agenda. The boundaries of the state are different than they were before, blurred and not as distinguishable, making it difficult to uncover where the state ends and civil society and the markets begin. Its functions also change because of the increasing power of the individual to set precedents government must follow thanks to tools such as human rights legislation and small business subsidies. The interconnectedness of this world requires formal oversight at the international level, including international standardization in line with the liberal notion of internationalism. As globalization continues to bring constant technological change and ever-greater interdependencies, there is a greater need to ensure a standardized system of protection.

Another major reason for this ever-increasing power of the individual is the fact that the language and framework of liberalism itself leads to greater empowerment of the individual, for to believe in political freedoms means that one has to accept the freedom of all other individuals.

These changes have all coalesced to bring about the current state of affairs, with people calling not for bigger government but better governments, not unregulated markets, but markets that are regulated where market failures would occur.

We are now seeing a new social contract that is being formed in the wake of the financial crisis. We have already seen a resurgence in state intervention and a return of Keynesian economics. Many have suggested this is the death of neoliberalism. In certain senses, this is true. We have seen that our freedoms can be threatened if we don't take concerted actions to think in the long term. We must also remember we are still living in a world more interconnected than ever before and even though this does increase uncertainty, it requires us to put in place long-term strategies to deal with these significant problems. Globalization has brought the world to a level of interconnectedness that has not been matched with a proper growth in global governance institutions that would be able to deal with a crisis of this magnitude.

STATE

With the major questioning of neoliberalism, people have started to question the unregulated marketplace. There has also been a re-emergence of state intervention. The call from the public is for bigger government to cede way to better government. We are now entering the era of the post-regulatory state, one that factors in the strategies of NGOs and businesses and is inclusive of public-private partnerships and smart government — incorporating the latest technologies into the work of government. These align directly with decentred regulation — designed by more than just the state. The work of its key proponent, Julia Black, is based in the idea that regulation should no longer be centred in the state but should arise out of various forces of influence, including those external to the state. Black currently teaches Regulation at the London School of Economics alongside Robert Baldwin and Martin Lodge.

At the core of the post-regulatory state is the idea it should no longer be the only regulatory body. A smart and effective state brings in businesses and civil society so it can alter things in a way not thought possible before. This causes different problems than were seen previously, notably accountability issues, as these bodies are not directly elected by the citizens of a country. The interaction between civil society and the government needs to continue and, moreover, be fostered and encouraged to become part of the regulatory process to further empower the individual. In the wake of the regulatory state, we are experiencing shifting states of being, where power is being diffused to more actors at both the sub-national and the global level. This diffusion of power from the state to other actors is occurring both vertically and horizontally.

One of the key functions for states emerging from this crisis is to ensure strong efforts to lower deficits, so as to protect the freedoms of future generations. This will require the state to trim the fat. It needs to cut out what is best left to the marketplace and civil society and to ensure proper amounts of funding to essential services. Before that, the state's first priority is making sure that all of those people who can work get the chance to work, which will help get society moving again and help build the infrastructure of the future — it could even create the green jobs needed to tackle the major problem of climate change. After that is finished and the recovery is secure, the government needs to aim to lower the deficit and to loosen its grip over the freedom of the nation.

This current financial crisis has also shown the world is globalized yet it is the nation state which is left trying to bail the institutions out. Greater global governance structures are needed. An American crisis was exported all around the world because of lack of structures. Reforms to correct for this at the global level are needed and will be discussed later, along with the underlying reasons they are needed. Should proper safeguards not be put in place, the burden will still rest with the state in the future. The state in the current era needs to ensure it does not seek to nationalize — this has been seen in history to be an ineffective solution. Government needs to stand against nationalization, just as strongly as it stands against a market that is being run incorrectly.

A smarter, more effective, more integrated state is called for in this new social contract. There is an opportunity for the state to use its power to make an effective change to protecting future freedoms, as well as pushing forward negative and positive freedoms to people both within the state and outside it. The state needs to live within its means and create the green jobs of the future. This smarter state has a role in extending freedoms not only within the state but across borders as well. This ultimately will define the role of the state.

MARKETS AND THE TWENTY-FIRST CENTURY ECONOMY

The foundation of this new economy must be based upon hard work, responsibility and accountability. Keynesian economics has made a resurgence, nationalization of banks has taken place in certain countries, stimulus plans were put into place — all of this because the markets collapsed, showing that an under-regulated free market does not serve the public interest. Markets are more integrated than ever before and a sub-prime mortgage crisis in America can affect the entire global financial system. We have seen the first crisis of globalization. Compensating for such things requires coordination and cooperation between regulators across borders. A major reason for the spread of the crisis was that the global institutions in place had weak rules and unclear mandates. A 21st Century market is one that works in the public interest with institutions governed by more stringent oversight requirements.

At the heart of the 21st Century market is economic freedom. Within a proper regulatory framework, this will create strong economic growth, opportunity, innovation and lift millions out of poverty. It is important to understand the major regulatory functions in this modern world need to embrace stricter oversight so as to understand how to preserve core system integrity, while still ensuring an efficient market that is transparent.

Ever since Adam Smith first laid out the idea of the invisible hand, our world has been progressively moving towards freer and freer markets. Within classical liberalism, a free market society was the central concept. This has always been an ethereal subject, a belief that somehow letting people go their own way and have complete freedom through the purity of self-interest will help society as a whole. This ideal has always led people to call for more power to the markets, more openness. In reality, greater freedom of the market has always gone hand-in-hand with greater regulation and oversight of the market, out of necessity. This liberalization of the markets is only set to continue, albeit with regulation to ensure market failures are accounted for as we have now seen the results of under-regulated markets. A new regulatory framework for the 21st Century is called for — a new Bretton Woods. It has been argued there has been a failure of the neoliberal model. What really needs to be ensured is that regulation does not become more hands-on. We should not turn to the failed idea of the completely centrally planned economy. Free markets have been a part of the liberal agenda ever since the concept of negative liberty took shape, and today there are more free markets around the world than ever before. The free market has produced more capital, more growth and more dynamism than any other economic system. We now understand that "Economic freedom is simply a requisite for political freedom. By enabling people to cooperate with one another without coercion or central direction it reduces the area over which political power is exercised."[93]

At the heart of this new society is the demand for a restructuring of the economy for the 21st Century. If done correctly, this economy will bring financial stability, create green jobs, run responsible budgets and ultimately tackle the long-term problems ignored for far too long. The amazing thing about these changes is that, if done correctly, they will not only benefit the long-term interests of a country but will also be a force for good in the short term.

This is not about scrapping the old economic model, it is about focusing on the most important parts. It is about reaffirming the concepts there is a dignity in work and through ethical approaches that the economy will work for the public interest. A key aspect of this new market is that it is a regulated market to protect freedoms, not to curtail them. A key body within this new framework of the market is the regulatory agency, upon which the proper functioning of the market hinges.

The marketplace needs to be tied to long-term results. This means executive pay should be attached to long-term thinking. The state also needs to foster the use of markets to produce a low-carbon economy through instruments such as a cap-and-trade system. Free-trade agreements need to be fostered because protectionism has been shown to be fatal to recovery and markets need to be opened. Such agreements increase economic growth, get the economy moving again and, in due course, bring back the high-wage, highly-skilled jobs liberal states depend upon. In poor areas, lack of property rights and essential services are the greatest inhibitors to wealth creation, which is why property rights are especially important in the fight against poverty and

---

93 Friedman, Milton; Friedman, Rose, *Free to Choose: A Personal Statement* (Harcourt Brace Jovanovich, 1980): 2-3.

need to be protected and enhanced alongside essential services — international agreements and trade have spurred such protections. The global structure of financial architecture needs to be cooperative and coordinated. Markets are global and regulation needs to be too, along the lines of the post-regulatory state. States need to cut back their deficits as soon as possible and restore fiscal responsibility for future generations.

A 21st century economy is one that rewards hard work, accountability and responsibility. A working market will be innovative, dynamic and produce strong economic growth. The financial crisis showed the damage of a marketplace that is not equipped with the proper regulatory system. Better regulation that tackles specific problems is called for, not simply more regulation. One key area of reform is making the market think long-term, meaning executive pay should not reward short-term prospects.

LOCAL

The financial crisis sparked a pull away from the local back to the state level. As the state starts reigning itself back in, as it is meant to do, there will be more room for individual activism. In recent years most action has taken place at the local level. Forward-looking action by individuals, as well as cities, has tackled such things as climate change and highlighted issues related to arts and culture and other activities in the social sphere, all with an eye to changing larger dynamics from the local level and all with the sense that the local level is the appropriate place for such change to take root.

We are now living in a period of time where the individual has the greatest chance in history to make a major difference, as there has been an unprecedented growth of civil society both because of the changes the state brought forth to grow civil society and through the natural growth of civil society itself. Civil society is now more listened to by the state and has greater ability to fill in the gaps at the global level where states are unable to. Still, more work must be done to empower the individual — individuals need greater freedom to start a small business, employment law needs further fine-tuning to ensure all people are treated equally regardless of their background and democracy must become more open, accountable and transparent, ultimately making it more inclusive of the individual.

Never before in history have individuals had the ability to affect government decisions as they do today. Never before in history have individuals had the ability to define themselves with so little opposition. Never before in history have individuals had to be so innovative and entrepreneurial as they have been called to do today and never before in history have people had the opportunity to be so innovative and entrepreneurial. This is the knowledge age, dependent on what lies between our ears to make this world a better place, to work and grow the economy, to turn the thinking of today into the actions of tomorrow through think tanks and NGOs and to create small businesses that are the lifeblood of our modern society. The empowerment of the individual is most fundamentally tied to the dignity of work. People respect and appreciate what work gives them — most people define their lives by their work, describing themselves as a teacher, a doctor, a stay-at-home mom or a hard-working labourer.

Greater recognition of the rights of women and others discriminated against in society must be fought for as integral to modern society. Income disparity between men and women and institutionalized discrimination both need to be addressed in a consistent manner. No matter what a person's background is, they must be able to get ahead. The law is the centrepiece of this shift, with employment law — notably anti-discrimination law — playing a key role in opening up opportunities for work. The ability for both the mother and father to find the time to raise their family in an equitable manner is a key area that still requires further expansion. Good parenting is one of the keys to unlocking the potential of the child, maximizing future freedoms. Promoting work-family balance means individuals are able to raise their families without worrying whether they will be laid off and out of work.

The individuals in their basement thinking of the next light bulb or steam engine need to be empowered to bring these innovations forward into the greater society. This is especially important to tackle climate change as green technologies and renewable energy systems need to extend from the ideas of innovative citizens. The world is also becoming more competitive, with innovation and creativity needed more than ever before — red tape and bureaucracy cannot stand in the way of a person creating a small business. Small businesses are the lifeblood of modern economies and need to have as few barriers as possible so that anyone with a bright idea can immediately put it to work.

Property rights are a key objective in ensuring the empowerment of individuals. They are likewise necessary to empower poor people around the world, notably through microfinance programs that help them to access financial services. Microfinance programs are meant to help create "a world in which as many poor and near-poor households as possible have permanent access to an appropriate range of high-quality financial services, including not just credit but also savings, insurance, and fund transfers."[94] Muhammad Yunus of Bangladesh was awarded a Nobel Peace Prize for his work in microfinance, through his Grameen Bank. Vancouver's credit union Vancity has shown that microfinance can be scaled up to work successfully in a wealthier society, with its peer-lending program having started numerous businesses. A lack of access to quality childcare is another issue holding back working families. The benefits are much greater than simply helping future generations cope while their parents are at work. People will be able to go to work and know their children are being taken care of. This security means that parents would not have to give up good opportunities that arise, that productivity would rise and that greater innovation can result. The economic

---

94 Christen, Robert Peck; Rosenberg, Richard; Jayadeva, Veena, *Financial institutions with a double-bottom line: implications for the future of microfinance* (CGAP Occasional Paper, 2004): 2-3.

growth of a country will increase as a result.[95] Truly, it is a net plus for individuals as well as society.

Democracy itself needs to be more inclusive of individuals in a more accountable and more transparent way as part of the greater fight against the democratic deficits that still exist. Government service programs, civic engagement and service to communities are specific areas where the state can foster such inclusivity and empower individuals.

Empowering individuals is also key to tackling poverty and crime. This is seen through such programs as Oportunidades in Mexico to give people goals, which in turn leads to receiving benefits on completion of those goals. This program provides a conditional cash transfer to families that are in need of government assistance. Conditions for this money include ensuring the children of a household attend school lessons, the family receives regular health check-ups and that the family has adequate nutrition. The money is paid directly to the mother who is responsible for ensuring the children go to school, receive the proper nutrition and go to health care clinics. Government data showed that 18.6% of Mexican households were listed under extreme poverty before the program was implemented, but only 15.8% in 2002 after the program was initiated.[96] It has not only decreased poverty, but has increased the levels of health and education where it is utilized. If you focus on youth in high-risk areas and empower them, there is far less chance of them displaying anti-social behaviour later on in life.

Our world is more interconnected than ever before — stars can be born on YouTube and old classmates and new work contacts alike can be kept informed about one's activities on Facebook. The internet has opened up new avenues of empowerment, with the expression of ideas onto a global platform and the ability for

95 Kimmel, Jean, "Child Care, Female Employment, and Economic Growth," *Journal of the Community Development Society*, Vol. 37, No. 2 (Summer 2006). http://economicdevelopmentandchildcare.org/documents/special_journal_issues/jcds/kimmel.pdf, retrieved August 4 2011.
96 Braine, Theresa, "Reaching Mexico's Poorest," *Bulletin of the World Health Organization* (2011): 593.

online social networks to influence political debate. The internet has truly further democratized our society but not everyone has access and this creates its own set of inequalities, which will be discussed later.

Individual empowerment has always been a key element of the liberal agenda, originally through the notion of keeping one from harming another, now growing to include the idea of positive freedoms and evolving to include future generations. These are seen as fundamental components of liberalism today.

GLOBAL

The global pull for power has never been seen to be as necessary as it is today. This is owed to the collapse of the global financial system being largely based in lack of coordination and cooperation on the part of global financial institutions. It must be remembered there are further global challenges in this world that demand their own institutions and their own responses.

After the financial crisis, the lack of global mechanisms in place to deal with the situation was made clear. This led leaders such as Gordon Brown, Prime Minister of the United Kingdom, to call for " . . . a new Bretton Woods — building a new international financial architecture for the years ahead . . . " During the Second World War, far-sighted leaders like Roosevelt and Churchill were already thinking about the framework that would be needed for the future," he said. "Whilst in the heat of the battle — taking steps to forge the reconstruction and peace that was to come . . . With the same courage and foresight of [these] founders, we must now reform the international financial system around the agreed principles of transparency, integrity, responsibility, good housekeeping and cooperation across borders."[97] It is clear across the board that the state should not be protectionist in a situation

---

97 Jackson, Guy, "World needs new Bretton Woods, says Brown," (Agence France-Presse, 2008). http://afp.google.com/article/ALeqM5iqbjATskwxNr2ty DViM7 bbz8J_rg, retrieved March 20, 2010.

such as this. This took place at the time of the Great Depression, which only prolonged the effects of the crisis. The G20 has taken it upon itself to become the key economic forum for these types of situations. This was an expansion of the longer-standing G8. However, there was the realization that even though financial transactions are global with global impacts, the only opportunity to bail out the financial institutions was necessarily at a state level, making it difficult to coordinate action across the board.

Another key area of focus at the global level is climate change. The UNFCCC meeting in Mexico produced only minimal results, following on the previous meeting at Copenhagen, which had produced even less in the way of results. The United Nations has been failing to keep its end of the bargain.

Looking at the UN in particular, David Held argues the UN needs to do two things to make the organization more fair. One is to find some way of financing itself that doesn't rely upon charity from the richest members. The second is to make it more inclusive of the public. This includes making the UN Secretariat more accountable and transparent. Held writes that "there is no clear division of labour among the myriad of international government agencies; functions often overlap, mandates frequently conflict and aims and objectives too often get blurred. There are a number of competing and overlapping organizations and institutions all of which have some stake in shaping global public policy".[98] The most compelling reform he suggests be put into place is the United Nations Parliamentary Assembly. This would seek to make the process more democratic and more accountable. This democratization of an international organization would be following the example set by institutions such as the European Union. Democratization of these global institutions has largely come in the footsteps of globalization. Globalization has just ploughed ahead, intertwining all of the market economies around the world. However, there has not been as resounding a success on

---

98 Held, David, *Cosmopolitanism: Ideals, Realities and Deficits* (Cambridge: Polity Press, 2010): 160

the part of global organizations to democratize, even in the wake of the global financial crisis. Globalization has not only produced an increase in calls for democratization, but has also increased the legitimacy of international law.

We are left with the current state of affairs, the current social contract. The state has taken on more power, at the expense of markets, while at the same time relying heavily upon civil society and non-state actors. Global architecture has not kept pace with the demands placed on it, despite a continual push for it to be reinvented to properly address such demands. The individual can also be seen to have more power to individually enact change than ever before in our society. It is from the individual the important issues of climate change were brought to the table, it is from individuals working through civil society that agendas are set and it is individuals who subsequently vote in democratic elections.

As greater integration of countries takes place, greater forms of global governance need to be put in place. Without the proper institutions, disastrous results will naturally follow and the state and the individual will both suffer. This occurred with the financial crisis and will be seen at many more turns without reform.

What can be taken from all of this is that what is called for is not bigger government, or smaller government, but good government. This means a government that can harness the talents of individuals who take part in international affairs as equals, understanding their own limits and the strengths of global cooperation, and understand it does have a role to help regulating the markets to ensure serious market failures are more unlikely to happen.

5

ROLE OF THE STATE

The twin pillars of New Liberalism envision a new role for the state in this world. Timeless freedom calls upon the state to not only continue its battle to extend the freedoms found under social liberalism but to extend those freedoms to future generations. The new social contract requires a smarter state, with power split among civil society, global institutions and the market economy. States still have an essential and integral role in ensuring freedom is extended to the greatest number of people throughout time. Specific examples that follow of what the state can do to extend freedom within the state and outside of the state are by no means meant to be exhaustive but illustrate key areas with which the state should be concerned. At the heart of this notion of New Liberal policy are three key objectives. Firstly, policy must seek to protect people from harm. Secondly, it must enhance opportunities of those it targets. Thirdly, it must do so within a sustainable framework that benefits our children and our grandchildren. The policies put in place should be those policies that are proven to work in practice and not those policies based solely upon ideology.

Freedoms discussed previously, climate change, fiscal responsibility and inequalities have to be dealt with both within the state and outside it. Timeless freedoms serve as a fundamental component of the new role of the state, but are only one piece of the puzzle. There are still further freedoms that need to be protected and extended. The state now is recognized to hold this positive duty to protect freedoms, which means the state has a positive role to play in this new world. This needs to be tempered by the remembrance its role is to only function where individuals can't and to trust in people wherever possible. Tied to this need to protect timeless freedoms is an increasing need to empower the individual as well as to work hard to establish the global bodies needed in order to bring peace and security, including financial.

This is why there has to be a continued focus on strengthening the rule of law, protecting services which enhance our freedom such as education and health care, continuing the struggle to bring about multicultural countries based in tolerance and respect for all cultures and communities, investing in the science and technology that will allow us to foresee future threats to our society and respecting the freer movement of people. The responsibilities of the state do not end at its own borders. There must be a realignment in understanding that a common humanity extends to all people on this planet. A conception of human security needs to be put into place, genocide anywhere needs to be prevented, terrorism needs to be dealt with, a world with less ability to start nuclear war needs to be pursued and peace needs to be the ultimate goal of any New Liberal. It is in this manner the state's primary purpose is to be an enabler of a free society. An exhaustive list of what the role of the state should be is beyond the scope of any book, but it can illustrate the areas in which the state does have a positive role in creating and extending freedoms to all peoples of all times.

It is fundamentally important that the leaders who claim support of liberalism actually believe in the limits to their own power and realize their duty is merely to be one player among many in extending freedom not only to the people living today but to future generations that will inhabit this planet.

ESSENTIAL SERVICES

To be a New Liberal means standing for the modernization of essential services, such as health care, education and a social safety net. The welfare system under New Liberalism focuses on giving individuals the tools to bounce back, as well as become self-reliant in doing so. This requires a continuing fight for welfare-to-work programs. Positive liberty starts as a role of the state providing the health care and education needed to allow the individual to develop as a person. This process continues. Reforms are needed to extend education to people in the form of early education and care, all the way up to higher education and job-training and retraining programs. Not only does timeless freedom call for the protection of freedoms of future generations, it also calls for the protection of the elderly in connection with our intergenerational contract and pension plans reforms. The state also has a large role to play in health care. Key reforms need to take place, including digitizing hospital records to make the system more efficient and save taxpayer dollars. There needs to be a focus on covering all citizens of a country, not only as a human right, but to make people more productive when they go to work. Healthy people are productive workers.

A strong safety net is needed to get people back on their feet after they fall into difficult times. These systems need to be built in such a way people do not become dependent on them and they serve their purpose for the most vulnerable who need the help, not those who abuse the system. These reforms are more necessary now than ever, with an aging population and shifting demographics.

The concept of the welfare state was a direct reaction to the events of the Great Depression. There were arguably measures before this time, such as when David Lloyd George sought the creation of national insurance contributions for health care and employment benefits. William Beveridge laid the foundations of the current welfare state, with the creation of Social Insurance and Allied Services in the UK in 1942. The program was created with his idea that "All people of working age should pay a weekly national insurance contribution. In return, benefits would be paid to people who were sick, unemployed, retired or widowed."[99] Out of this report came the National Health Service and the Universal Child Benefit. The National Insurance Act, National Assistance Act and National Health Service Act were all passed in support of this report and Beveridge's idea of tackling the five 'giants': want, disease, ignorance, squalor and idleness.[100] These welfare institutions have been facing growing difficulties recently due to aging populations, the strains of the financial crisis and the growing size of their budgets. To tackle this, there needs to be a focus on reforming the institutions to adapt them to the 21st Century, most notably in three key areas: education, health care and pension plans.

The major guarantee for education needs to be quality teaching from the early stages of life through to post-secondary and job-training programs. The right to education is guaranteed worldwide in the United Nations' International Covenant on Economic, Social and Cultural Rights of 1966, Article 13. There is no greater ladder for social mobility than that of education. Economists have shown higher rates of education are needed in order to achieve high economic growth. Early education is fundamentally important because it not only allows the child to gain the skills they need from an early age but serves as a tool of empowerment that can unlock the potential of a child. Such skills are instrumental to the knowledge economy of the future and also enable children from any background, including those born into poverty, to be more socially mobile. Early childhood is one of the most important periods of development, defined roughly as the time between birth and the age of eight. Tied to this concept of early education is childcare. Not only will improvements in childcare enable early education, but they will also serve to increase the size of the economy by enabling both parents to work if they need to, without needing to worry about finding someone to watch over their children.

---

99 *Social Insurance and Allied Services* (Beveridge Report, 1942).
100 *Social Insurance and Allied Services* (Beveridge Report, 1942).

At the very heart of the education system are the teachers. Teachers have the ability to singularly change lives and set our future generations on the path to opportunity and success. With this in mind, the system needs to start rewarding the strongest teachers and ensuring high standards across the board. With strong teaching, the economy of the future will be stronger, there will be more innovation and creativity than ever before and there will ultimately be a better, more peaceful world. The state also needs to expand financial aid so whoever works hard and wants an education or job-training has the opportunity to pursue it. Education fits within the three key objectives of New Liberalism through a reduction of harm and criminal activity, an increase in opportunities towards equality and an ability to break the poverty trap.

The most fundamental concept of health care reform is ensuring it is affordable, both for the individual as well as the state. The key way to cut costs is to invest more in prevention of illnesses. Another avenue to cut costs is digitizing health records, which will also make the system more efficient — we have the technology for this, we just need to put it into practice. The populace will suffer if health care is not broad enough to cover all of its citizens. Two major goals of governments in the 21st Century are to improve access by shortening wait times and improving quality of care.

Looking specifically at the varying models of health care in the world we see that even the United States of America, which has opposed health care reform for one hundred years, has recently passed a bill expanding coverage to thirty-two million more Americans. In Canada, national health care service as implemented by the Liberal Party is almost completely publicly funded, one of the few remaining services of that sort. Most countries need to improve their focus on the prevention of problems, giving it equal weight to dealing with them after they arise, which will save a lot of money.

A health care plan, at its heart, is a plan to protect people from harm and to correct harm done. Health care naturally opens up opportunities by allowing people to work again. The aim must now be to make these systems sustainable so they aren't crushed under rising budget costs, aging populations and the financial crisis. Sustainability must be focused on in 21st Century policy development.

The purpose of pension plans is to keep the promise of the contract we have with older generations and younger generations in turn have with us to ensure the dignity and security of people who have devoted their working life to the economy of the country — the intergenerational contract. People have worked hard for their living and they have put their children through university — they have paid the bills and they deserve to retire in dignity. One policy area that needs to be addressed is the retirement age. Many people find reward in doing their work and do not want to be told when they have to retire — the retirement age should be moved up to allow them more choice. Granting older workers more freedom to choose when to leave the workforce will help the economy as the population ages by reducing the strain on public pension plans as it adds to the economy. This responsibility does not only stop at the state — every individual will need to make sure they save enough for retirement so society does not have to pay the bill. Immigration is also an important tool in ensuring the continuance of this system by bringing in younger workers to help compensate for the growing proportion of the population drawing pension benefits. This has the added benefit of fostering a multicultural community if the state addresses its functions properly.

Where an economic downturn sparks a need for jobs, we have seen governments will intervene, be they conservative or liberal. Another area that needs to be focused on is the minimum wage — the social contract of liberalism demands that those who work be able to make a living wage. Retraining programs allow those who lose a job because of the shifts in the economy to find another one with the aim of guaranteeing a wage they can actually use to support themselves. Employment insurance helps people get back on their feet when the rug is pulled out from under them — this is meant to to help people get back to work and its success should be measured by how many people leave it and not how many people enter it. As a risk system, such benefits are meant to help people when they are down on their luck but are willing to apply hard work and perseverance to make it back to work, not to enable people to become dependent upon it or abuse it. New Liberalism stresses that people who want to work should be able to work and be paid a living wage.

Investing in these essential services will open up freedom and opportunity for the state's citizens, reduce poverty, save money and in fact grow the economy, all while ensuring our intergenerational contract is fulfilled.

MULTICULTURALISM

No system in the world better protects and enhances diversity than the liberal model. Liberalism is founded upon the ideal all humans are born equal regardless of their ethnicity. In a modern global economy, it is necessary to find the best from wherever they originate and societies which are most open to citizens of the world will be the ones to reap the rewards. The country with the most tolerant and peaceful society will truly be the global leaders of the 21st Century. Multiculturalism, first instituted as public policy by the Canadian government in 1971, is an approach demanded by the effects of globalization. A society that adopts multiculturalism will flourish based upon the diversity within its own borders. The key is to balance tolerance with the concept of shared values within a country.

At the heart of multiculturalism is a respect for culture itself. The individual is most free when free to celebrate his or her culture — or that of others — as the ability to make cultural choices rather than be bound by them is essential to the freedom of the indivi-ual. "[Joseph] Raz insists the autonomy of individuals — their ability to make good choices amongst good lives — is intimately tied up with access to their culture, with the prosperity and flourishing of their culture and with the respect accorded their culture by others. Minority rights help ensure this cultural flourishing and mutual respect."[101]

Many have put forward that multiculturalism erodes the national identity of the citizens within the country. This is widely seen to be false. The concept of multiculturalism has strengthened identity, based upon a liberal nationalism that sees a country not based around ethnicity, but rather around something greater — a sense of community between all people living within a territory. Liberal nationalism is centred on the idea national symbols are not based on ethnicity, but upon shared values among the inhabitants within a country's borders with these national symbols up to the individual to accept or reject, engaging all citizens in the definition of their country.

The three-stage application of protection from harm, enhancing opportunities and enabling a better future directly applies to the concept of multiculturalism, the very purpose of which is to protect individuals from harm, as the dominant majority culture found in the political institutions could harm the minority cultures within that country if safeguards aren't put in place.

Why protect minority rights in the first place? Will Kymlicka, a professor at Queen's University in Canada and one of the leading scholars on multiculturalism, answers it by saying "by identifying the many ways that mainstream institutions are not neutral but rather are implicitly or explicitly tilted towards the interests and identities of the majority group . . . bias creates a range of burdens, barriers, stigmatizations and exclusions for members of minority groups which can only or best be remedied by minority rights"[102] and "by emphasizing the importance of certain interests which have typically been ignored by liberal theories of justice — e.g. interests in recognition, identity, language and cultural membership. If these interests are ignored or trivialized by the

---

101 Kymlicka, Will, *Politics in the Vernacular: Nationalism, Multiculturalism, Citizenship* (Oxford: Oxford University Press, 2001): 21.
102 Kymlicka, *Will, Politics in the Vernacular: Nationalism, Multiculturalism, Citizenship* (Oxford: Oxford University Press, 2001): 32.

state, then people will feel harmed — and indeed will be harmed — even if their civil, political and welfare rights are respected."[103] Since, as Kymlicka posits, "mainstream institutions are biased in favour of the majority, and the effect of this bias is to harm important interests related to personal agency and identity,"[104] therefore, "recognizing minority rights would actually strengthen solidarity and promote political stability by removing the barriers and exclusions which prevent minorities from wholeheartedly embracing political institutions."[105]

Multiculturalism also inherently enhances opportunities for all citizens within the country. It adds to economic growth and the moral well-being of a nation. Multiculturalism is the only way forward in this increasingly integrated world and it is also the greatest way to unlocking innovation and dynamism in the system as people hailing from a variety of cultures will bring fresh perspectives to every matter. There is a unity in diversity that is sought within the system of New Liberalism. Multiculturalism is about supporting and fostering diversity. This is strong economically as it produces innovation and economic growth. In a globalized world, you will have an advantage as more people move and travel, as the most harmonious society will be the most attractive. As accessible transportation increases immigration around the world, the country most suitable to this new era will be able to command the future. At the same time as immigrants bring different perspectives, emigrants forge connections around the world. India has noted the importance of emigrants from their country, offering 'Overseas Citizen of India' status as well as 'Person of Indian Origin status', the former guaranteeing all rights of citizenship other than political rights (voting).

Looking specifically at what the state can do, its core functions still come down to classical liberalism. "In all liberal democracies,

---

103 Kymlicka, *Will, Politics in the Vernacular: Nationalism, Multiculturalism, Citizenship* (Oxford: Oxford University Press, 2001): 32.

104 Kymlicka, *Will, Politics in the Vernacular: Nationalism, Multiculturalism, Citizenship* (Oxford: Oxford University Press, 2001): 36.

105 Kymlicka, *Will, Politics in the Vernacular: Nationalism, Multiculturalism, Citizenship* (Oxford: Oxford University Press, 2001): 36.

one of the major mechanisms for accommodating cultural differences is the protection of the civil and political rights of individuals. It is impossible to overstate the importance of freedom of association, religion, speech, mobility and political organization for protecting group difference."[106] The role the state should take in laying the framework for a multicultural society is an important one. At its foundation is the legal concept of minority rights. States should enable cultural events and minority-language newspapers, television and other media, while also passing laws which support minority rights. The state's role is positive because it broadens minds, allowing citizens to see everyone has the same hopes and dreams and, in doing so, gain empathy and learn a rich history. It also helps connect us to a sense of our common humanity and the idea we all have a stake in one another. It is not merely the state that needs to adopt change but the political parties that hope to steer it: "one way to reform the process is to make political parties more inclusive by reducing the barriers which inhibit women, ethnic minorities or the poor from becoming party candidates or party leaders."[107]

What needs to be clear when discussing minority rights is "It is clear that some kinds of minority rights would undermine rather than support, individual autonomy."[108] Kymlicka argues there are 'bad' minority rights and 'good' minority rights. Bad rights are those which seek to prevent individuals from going against traditional practices and customs. Good rights, on the other hand, are those that seek to prevent external pressures on society for citizens to give up their cultural identity. These are addressed by liberal culturalism, the idea that different cultures should be allowed to express their identity freely with the recognition that

---

106 Kymlicka, Will (1995) *Multicultural Citizenship: A Liberal Theory of Minority Rights* (Oxford: Oxford University Press, 2001): 26.

107 Kymlicka, Will, "Justice and Minority Rights" reprinted from *Multicultural Citizenship* (Oxford: Clarendon Press, 1995) in *Contemporary Political Philosophy: An Anthology*, ed. Robert E. Goodin and Philip Pettit (Oxford: Blackwell Publishing, 2006): 26-33, 108-130.

108 Kymlicka, Will, *Politics in the Vernacular: Nationalism, Multiculturalism, Citizenship* (Oxford: Oxford University Press, 2001): 22.

these views cannot be imposed on others in the community. "We can say that minority rights are consistent with liberal culturalism if a) they protect the freedom of individuals within the group; and b) they promote relations of equality (non-dominance) between groups."[109] There is a clear distinction between the freedom of an individual to celebrate their culture and the protection of traditions and customs that are imposed on people, most notably women.

A country that protects and supports diversity within its borders will have a more creative, more innovative and the more forward-looking state. This is the direction globalization demands and those states that stick to homogeneous paths will not be able to take advantage of the benefits that will come from a truly 21st Century approach.

SCIENCE AND TECHNOLOGY

Nothing has created more freedoms or provided the greatest threat to freedoms than science and technology. Technology has enabled us to communicate faster, express a stronger opinion, overcome propaganda and ultimately change our entire way of life. Technology has also revolutionized the ability to bring about social change. This was clearly seen in the Obama campaign of 2008 through the creation of a grassroots movement based upon internet tools and programs. This new ability to empower individuals through the power of the internet and the exchange of ideas is the future. At the same time, it has inhibited privacy, it has created more dangers to our freedoms in the realm of cyber-security and nuclear bombs present one of the most serious threats to our society.

The key way to grow knowledge in society is to go back to the fundamentals — protect freedom of speech. When basic rights are in place, knowledge can be shared, tested, argued and pushed forward. Intellectual property laws provide an example with

---

109 Kymlicka, Will, *Politics in the Vernacular: Nationalism, Multiculturalism, Citizenship* (Oxford: Oxford University Press, 2001): 23.

patents, which secure the right to an invention given to the creator in return for publicly disclosing it. These fundamental freedoms are essential for the scientific and technological community to function.

Without science we would not know that climate change is happening, without technology we would not have been able to be as productive as we are as a society, increasing both positive and negative freedoms. One only needs to look at history to understand the importance of government investing in technology. It was an investment in a railway that united Canada from sea to sea. It was investment in the internet that has lead to the fast-paced society we now live in.

Scientific research allows us to understand future threats to our freedoms. and can lead to breakthrough discoveries that cure diseases and ensure longer lifespans. Investment needs to begin right at the school level, investing in teachers of science who can produce the next generation of talent. Most importantly, the state should focus on providing the grants necessary for direct research. The Intergovernmental Panel on Climate Change helped focus the attention of the world on a major threat to our future.

Technological innovation can unlock dreams and imaginations. Sending a human to the moon was thought impossible. BlackBerry is now commonly used, and it was started with the aid of the federal government of Canada and the provincial government of Ontario. This piece of technology has made businesses more efficient, improved communication standards and changed how the workplace functions, by allowing people to work from wherever they are. Technology has enabled a great freedom of movement, where we can fly all around the world. Technology enables us to communicate more freely than ever before. These abilities all arose from government investment.

Government needs to invest in the availability of broadband networks to rural, poor and otherwise marginalized citizens. Investment in broadband networks can help improve economic development as well as helping to deal with the digital divide, one of the most serious equality problems our current society faces.

Where individuals do not have access to information technology based upon their income, location, gender or race, a gap in knowledge and skills takes place. Broadband access needs to be improved. Education is similarly needed to tackle this knowledge divide and to create the technologies of tomorrow. Individuals also need access to computers and alternative access to the internet where and when broadband is not available.

Science and technology can be one of the greatest forces for good in this world, helping explain future threats, opening up unimaginable future realities and serving as an integral feature of economic growth. Technology can protect us from harm, from nuclear threats to climate change. It enhances our opportunities by allowing the empowerment of individuals like never before.

RULE OF LAW

"The first condition of free government is government not by arbitrary determination of the ruler but by fixed rules of law, to which the ruler himself is subject."[110]

Where people do not follow the rule of law, a proper criminal justice system needs to be in place in order to maintain social order. Liberalism is meant to enhance freedom of the individual and, as crime is a direct threat to individual freedoms, New Liberalism stands against crime in a tough and measured way. Anything less and the freedoms of individuals everywhere will be jeopardized.

The state needs to defend the political and social order and it needs to maintain a functioning government in order to ensure and enhance the freedoms of the people it serves. It is important to get right down to the root causes of crime and to break the deviant behavioural deadlock that can be passed on to children. A criminal policy under New Liberalism needs to be tough on extremists to protect from harm but it needs to go hand-in-hand with enhanced opportunities through crime prevention and juvenile programs.

110 Hobhouse, L.T., *Liberalism* (Middlesex: The Echo Library, 2009): 11

These will enable children and grandchildren to break out of the criminal cycle fostered by their parents.

Order is a key component to our society — this is the purpose of the social contract in the first place. The legal system has evolved throughout the ages to ensure social order and stability. John Locke put forward that this rule of law needs to apply to all citizens, including the monarch — applying liberal views to what had been the province of the state, enforced at its whim. While the law serves as the rules behind the system, the police are the officers who enforce that law.

Police are at the frontline of freedom, justice and social order. They are the heroes of a free society and should be treated as such. Their position is to ensure the rule of law is upheld, including protecting property and ensuring social order. Dealing with crime in an effective manner is key to freedoms. Criminal law is really at its heart a legal form of the harm principle. While the police are the frontline of the system, justice can be also found in the courtroom. The courts serve a key function as the adjudicator of legal disputes and this is where an individual's rights are found.

It is interesting to note the greatest punishments liberal democracies hand out are deprivations of life, liberty and property, the fundamental freedoms. The state has to move beyond merely finding criminals, putting them through the court system and throwing them into prison. There needs to be a focus on preventing crime, as it will be less expensive in the long term and will lead to fewer victims. Youth who are at risk need to be a major focus, not only for their own sake, but for the sake of those who might end up their victims. Throughout the entire process from enforcement of laws to prosecution of crimes, there needs to be a re-affirmation of human rights.

Liberalism has at its heart a role for the rule of law — a system of law and order that is built around the concept of the harm principle but includes a role for enhancing opportunities and breaking the cycle of at-risk youth to create a better future for all.

DEMOCRATIC DEFICITS

Both within the state and outside of the state, democratic deficits are a major roadblock to freedom. These democratic deficits touch both developed and developing countries alike. Where developed countries have corruption and backroom deals, developing countries can have weak states and weak societies. We see a growth in terrorism and genocide within the states that have weak democratic infrastructure. Therefore, moving forward is not only about states extending freedoms within but it is also about states seeking out ways to extend these freedoms to others.

Democratic deficits need to be combatted in order to protect us from the inherent harm caused by a malfunctioning democracy. A proper liberal democracy is the greatest system known to enhance opportunities and freedoms of its individuals. Enabling a better future requires long-term democratic structures to be geared to tackle long-term democratic problems. The House of Lords in the United Kingdom or the Senate in Canada are long-term legislative bodies, not subject to regular elections, which allow a focus on longer-term priorities in a bipartisan fashion.

A fundamental problem with people in political positions is their ability to make corrupt bargains. Corruption can take on several different forms: nepotism, cronyism and bribery among others. Bribery alone accounts for over a trillion dollars world-wide. Cronyism is where those in power place friends in positions of authority, while nepotism is more related to special treatment of family and friends — these are harder to put a monetary value on.

To counteract corruption, there needs to be respect for basic freedoms. There also needs to be accountability and transparency mechanisms built into government, a strong rule of law and a strong civic society. A liberal democracy will push for less and less corruption, as it inherently relies upon the opposite. Corruption destroys the ability for essential services to be delivered in a timely fashion. The lack of economic freedoms is the root cause of corruption. Therefore, enhancing liberal democratic freedoms within countries can root out corruption. Increasing transparency requires opening meetings to the public and to the press. Eliminating revolving doors for lobbyists to gain special access to promote certain agendas over the will and needs of the people is also integral to inhibiting corruption in government.

Ending democratic deficits requires different policies for different countries in different situations. The aim should always be a more transparent, open and fairly elected government that appoints people based on merit.

Human Security and Genocide

Human security is the idea that security should be focused on the individual and not on the state. The first priority is to change the conception there is national security. Security is meant to focus around the individual.

The United Nations Development Programme's 1994 *Human Development Report* stated the best way to make a more secure world was to provide a 'freedom from fear' and 'freedom from want'. Freedom from fear correlates with classical liberalism, where freedom from want correlates with social liberalism. The report lays out seven areas where human security should be extended, the first being economic security. This works directly along the lines of social liberalism, arguing that an individual should be able to earn a living and where that is not possible, to be covered under a social safety net. Where this is not the case, conflict and tensions start to appear. Health security is deeply connected with the concept of the safety net. Environmental security tracks nicely with New Liberalism. Personal security includes security from the state. Community security addresses your right to your own culture and value system. Political security is the protection of human rights. The whole idea of human security can trace itself to the founding notions of liberalism — that we only give up certain freedoms in order to have security for ourselves, not security for the state. This also aligns well with the notion of human rights and the idea that our human dignity is founded upon these freedoms.

One of the fundamental differences between human security and the traditional notion of security is that it puts violence against women at the heart of the agenda. It is often women who are most affected by conflicts yet the traditional notion of security does not in any way deal with that reality. The other major difference is that human security states there is a responsibility to prevent, react and rebuild, which goes far beyond the traditional boundaries of security. Two major examples of this extended from the hand of former Canadian Minister of Foreign Affairs Lloyd Axworthy who successfully applied the concept of human security to the creation of the Ottawa Treaty banning anti-personnel landmines and was nominated for the Nobel Peace Prize for those efforts. Axworthy then helped create the 'responsibility to protect', along with future Liberal leader Michael Ignatieff, which set out that states have a responsibility to protect its citizens from 'mass atrocity crimes', cited as genocide, war crimes, crimes against humanity and ethnic cleansing — and further that the international community has a responsibility to intervene when a state fails to offer such protection. A ban on anti-personnel landmines was called for because of the grave collateral damage that continues after the conflicts in which they are used. In fact, the United Nations has estimated these landmines can be as ten times more likely to injure and kill civilians than soldiers.

The responsibility to protect was sought because genocide anywhere is a threat to freedom everywhere. The very idea a person can be targeted based upon tribalism must be fought against. The set of principles established prevents states from using force but sets out a legal obligation to use diplomatic, economic and other peaceful means to stop mass atrocity crimes.[111] States can however use the Security Council Collective Security measures to stop genocide. The Security Council Collective Security system works alongside states using their soft powers to prevent genocide. In extreme cases, the principles allow for military intervention,

---

111 Kalkman, Matthew, "Responsibility To Protect: A Bow Without An Arrow," *Cambridge Student Law Review* Vol. 5, No. 1 (Cambridge, 2009).

but only through the authority of the Security Council and the General Assembly of the United Nations.

The role of the state in dealing with genocide is severely limited by law. Within the UN Charter, Article 2(4) sets out that "All Members shall refrain in their international relations from the threat or use of force against the territorial integrity or political independence of any state or in any other manner inconsistent with the Purposes of the United Nations".[112]

The restriction on the use of force by the state is straightforward, with only two exceptions to this, self-defence under Article 51 of the UN Charter and collective security. Article 51 states that "Nothing in the present Charter shall impair the inherent right of individual or collective self-defence if an armed attack occurs against a Member of the United Nations . . . ".[113] Collective security is found in Chapter VII of the Charter of the United Nations, where Article 39 states that "The Security Council shall determine the existence of any threat to the peace, breach of the peace, or act of aggression and shall make recommendations, or decide what measures shall be taken in accordance with Articles 41 and 42, to maintain or restore international peace and security."[114]

This boils down to the state needing to work through the UN Security Council to address such problems. Genocide policies have at their heart the idea that freedoms need to be constantly extended, even by states beyond the borders within which the genocide occurs.

Arguably, an emerging duty of care is placed upon states to use diplomatic, economic and other peaceful means to prevent genocide. Genocide represents everything liberalism is not. It represents group thinking and group mentality whereby individuals are not accepted as equals and are not given the same chances for freedom. Genocide also represents a turning point in the history of the concept of security. The liberal concept of human security has shifted the focus from the state to the individual.

---

112 Charter of the United Nations (1945), Article 2(4).
113 Charter of the United Nations (1945), Article 51.
114 Charter of the United Nations (1945), Article 39.

TERRORISM

Terrorism has been one of the greatest threats to freedom since the 21st Century began, inherently trying to stop freedoms humans are born with. Its method is not to target everyone but symbols such as buildings or the innocent, such as women and children. Terrorists pretend to speak out on behalf of communities but the actions are taken by individuals who prioritize their own goals above the security of others. It does not make sense to argue that we are all unique and different and then attack the opposition as singular. This is why a solution can only be found through making allies in the regions where terrorism is found and working together to root out the extremists.

A three-stage test ascertains whether a government is tough on extremists. Firstly, an effective program should protect citizens from harm, particularly one that enhances opportunities in those regions known to produce a high level of terrorism. Secondly, lack of freedom of development is a known trigger of terrorism and radicalization — efforts must be made to address starvation, lack of education and lack of health services, among other things. Thirdly, enhancing opportunities will ensure people don't fall into terrorism — democratic deficits of weak or failed states must be fought with measures that extend opportunity to people in those states, so individuals see less reason to turn to extremism. A policy that takes a strong stance against extremists while spreading opportunity will further enable a better future by relieving international tensions.

As the Madrid Agenda states, "Democratic principles and values are essential tools in the fight against terrorism. Any successful strategy for dealing with terrorism requires terrorists to be isolated. Consequently, the preference must be to treat terrorism as criminal acts to be handled through existing systems of law enforcement and with full respect for human rights and the rule of law."[115] Its recommendations include "taking effective

---

115 Amnesty International, "Counter-terrorism and criminal law in the EU," (2005).

measures to make impunity impossible either for acts of terrorism or for the abuse of human rights in counter-terrorism measures" and "the incorporation of human rights laws in all anti-terrorism programmers and policies of national governments as well as international bodies." Seeing terrorism as a war has been a failure in the reaction of states to terrorism when counter-terrorism is more properly viewed as a law-enforcement issue as put forward by former Secretary of State Colin Powell, which would have attained far better results. Labelling terrorism as a war and treating it as a war often makes enemies of allies and strangers of friends. A whole culture should not be demonized because of the actions of a few.

There is no universally agreed definition of terrorism. The US military defines counter-terrorism as "Operations that include the offensive measures taken to prevent, deter, preempt and respond to terrorism."[116] Anti-terrorism on the other hand is "Defensive measures used to reduce the vulnerability of individuals and property to terrorist acts, to include limited response and containment by local military and civilian forces."[117] Dealing with terrorism in the system of human security means attacking it at its root source. Past a strong stance on extremism and the enhancement of opportunity, proper intelligence is needed to counteract terrorism. Proper technology to gather intelligence can stop attacks from taking place and the state should continue to invest in technology and maintain top-of-the-line science, ensure that its intelligence agencies are adequately funded and apply economic sanctions to known terrorist groups.

Fighting terrorism requires all of the freedoms liberalism espouses. Terrorists win the moment we fail to follow our values. The duty to protect benefits all our freedoms, as they all are tied together. Increasing funding of technology improves society in general, counteracts terrorism and helps make essential services

---

116 US Department of Defense, "Joint Publication 1-02 Department of Defense Dictionary of Military and Associated Terms" (12 July 2007).
117 US Department of Defense, "Joint Publication 1-02 Department of Defense Dictionary of Military and Associated Terms" (12 July 2007).

more efficient. By counteracting terrorism and providing essential services, we foster peace. Being tough on extremists is a necessity in order to provide security to those they threaten, which goes hand-in-hand with extending opportunities to those they try to corrupt.

Nuclear Disarmament

Nuclear power has many safety considerations arising from natural disasters, accidents and those seeking to use its energy to cause destruction and create fear. It both serves as a source of energy in a world that may be running low on fossil fuels and presents the grave threat of potential annihilation. Nuclear weapons cannot offer the former but certainly threaten the latter.

It is important to reassess the size of the world stockpile as we enter a new era of nuclear war — the era of nuclear terrorism and non-governmental proliferation. It is important to reassess the size of the world stockpile, as we not only continue to face the growing threat of nuclear proliferation, but also the growing threat of nuclear terrorism in this new era. The old theories of Mutually Assured Destruction, or MAD, that served their purpose during the Cold War no longer apply. In the post 9/11 world, we have seen the damage that terrorism can bring and that this new nuclear age doesn't follow the same rules as the Cold War. Fear of nuclear attack is no longer just about war between superpowers, but also non-state actors accessing weapons. This is a direct threat to the peace and security of people around the world. A policy of nuclear disarmament inherently protects from harm caused by nuclear weapons, but is limited to states and global agreements. Peace and security are preconditions for enhanced opportunities to take place, so we must find ways to prevent the spread of nuclear weapons. A world without nuclear war is a sustainable world.

One only needs to look at the devastation and destruction caused in Hiroshima and Nagasaki to understand the horrors of the nuclear weapon. Tsutomu Yamaguchi (1916–2010), the sole officially-recognized survivor of both Hiroshima and Nagasaki, said "The reason that I hate the atomic bomb is because of what it does to the dignity of human beings."[118] He wrote that after the bomb was dropped the people looked like "ant-walking alligators ... were now eyeless and faceless — with their heads transformed into blackened alligator hides displaying red holes, indicating mouths."[119] Yamaguchi continued, "The alligator people did not scream. Their mouths could not form the sounds. The noise they made was worse than screaming. They uttered a continuous murmur — like locusts on a midsummer night. One man, staggering on charred stumps of legs, was carrying a dead baby upside-down."[120] The devastating effects on these two cities need to be a constant reminder of what can be unleashed.

Countries that have nuclear weapons and admitted testing them include the United States, Russia, France, the UK, the People's Republic of China, India, Pakistan and North Korea. Over the years there have been several attempts to control nuclear weapons, through the International Atomic Energy Agency, through the Nuclear Non-Proliferation Treaty and through the Comprehensive Nuclear-Test-Ban Treaty. Bilateral treaties under SALT and START between the US and Russia have also served to limit nuclear proliferation. A new treaty called New START has been ratified by the US and Russia and seeks to half the number of strategic launchers for nuclear weapons. It seeks to reduce the number of long-range nuclear warheads by thirty percent from the previous SORT treaty (also known as the Treaty of Moscow), as well as creating a new inspection and verification regime.

With traditional nuclear powers reducing their stockpiles, the major nuclear threat in the 21st Century is nuclear terrorism. The possibility of nuclear weapons falling into the hands of a terrorist

118 Robbins, M W, ed.,. "Japanese Engineer Survived Atomic Strike on Hiroshima and Nagasaki," *Military History Magazine* (Weider History Group, August/September 2009): 8.

119 Pellegrino, Charles R., *The Last Train from Hiroshima: The Survivors Look Back* (New York: Henry Holt and Co., 2010).

120 Pellegrino, Charles R., *The Last Train from Hiroshima: The Survivors Look Back* (New York: Henry Holt and Co., 2010).

has increased, owing to technology and availability following the dissolution of the Soviet Union. A nuclear terrorist can be described as someone who "uses in any way radioactive material . . . with the intent to cause death or serious bodily injury,"[121] according to the 2005 United Nations International Convention for the Suppression of Acts of Nuclear Terrorism. Osama bin Laden is known to have said before his death that he wanted an American Hiroshima. The materials already exist for terrorists to purchase on the black market. The Cold War search for peace was through MAD, however, we are now living in different times. Mutually Assured Destruction meets its match with nuclear terrorism, as a terrorist expects to die in an attack and doesn't care what happens after and there is no direct target to counteract if the source is a violent non-state player. MAD no longer applies the way it once did, so a new concept of security is needed in relation to nuclear weapons — disarmament itself.

Nuclear proliferation is the other major threat, one that has significantly caused power struggles in North Korea and Iran. Nuclear proliferation now centres on the spread of nuclear weapons and materials to countries that are not 'Nuclear Weapons States' under the Nuclear Nonproliferation Treaty. These countries that build nuclear weapons outside of the safeguards and legality of the treaty pose considerable risk to humanity as they are much more likely to be meant as tools of destruction and war.

At the beginning, nuclear disarmament campaigners started to appear in only certain pockets, with calls for an international oversight body. It was a decade before the movement started to gain momentum which grew in response to nuclear testing and the resulting fallout. Nuclear fallout is the radiation that comes from a nuclear explosion — this can result in quick death, slow mutations and radiation poisoning, among other things. One need not be present for the explosion to suffer the results — the resultant radioactive dust can cause contamination in the food chain and persist for years. The Partial Test Ban responded to protests in

---

121 United Nations International Convention for the Suppression of Acts of Nuclear Terrorism, Article 2 (Nuclear Terrorism Convention, 2005).

a limited fashion by prohibiting nuclear testing other than that done underground.

Nuclear explosions pose a clear threat to our future, one more brutal, more deadly and with longer-lasting negative impacts than any other weapon. A device the size of a traditional bomb can wipe out an entire city. Hiroshima and Nagasaki remain the only times nuclear bombs have been used in an aggressive manner.

International law states that the threat or use of force is illegal, including the Geneva Conventions, the Hague Conventions, the UN Charter and the Universal Declaration of Human Rights. The bar for the use of nuclear weapons is even higher, as evidenced in *Legality of the Threat or Use of Nuclear Weapons,* an advisory opinion delivered by the International Court of Justice on July 8th, 1996: "the threat or use of nuclear weapons would generally be contrary to the rules of international law applicable in armed conflict and in particular the principles and rules of humanitarian law. In view of the current state of international law and of the elements of fact at its disposal, the Court cannot conclude definitively whether the threat or use of nuclear weapons would be lawful or unlawful in an extreme circumstance of self-defence, in which the very survival of a State would be at stake."[122]

The state has a role to oppose nuclear proliferation and nuclear terrorism and also to push for decreasing the size of current stockpiles through the use of economic sanctions and diplomatic pressure.

PEACE AND SECURITY

Peace is the highest goal of New Liberalism. Inherently, peace represents the truest freedom one can have in society. It extends itself through every goal of liberalism, from the most basic understandings of political and economic freedoms to the need for human security or through easing tensions over oil — one of

---

122 "Legality of the Threat or Use of Nuclear Weapons," Advisory Opinion of 8 July 1996 — General List No. 95, section 1 (1995–1998).

the great threats to future peace is a world with limited oil but a large demand among nations, which could serve to precipitate war. Liberalism's thrust towards peace extends from the thinking of Adam Smith — that as nation-states industrialized, war would become too costly and free markets would lead to world peace — onwards to modern views of liberalism. Without security there can be no peace. At the core of liberalism, the ideal of freedom — true freedom — is based upon cooperation and peace. Peace and security inherently protects from harm, enhances opportunities and enables a better future.

The very principles implemented for New Liberalism have been shown to alleviate tensions through history, whether it is the greater integration of world economies, providing for the basic necessities of life or addressing energy security put at risk by shrinking oil reserves. Internationally, states need to increase diplomacy and multilateralism in world affairs to consistently aim for peace. The military needs to be geared towards the responsibility to protect and human security around the globe. The framework of the United Nations needs to be strengthened as it remains our greatest potential forum to work for peace.

Strengthening the United Nations is key to long-term peace and security, part of the greater view of liberal internationalism. Liberal internationalism "lays a special claim to what world politics is and can be: a state of peace."[123] One function of the UN towards this end is peacekeeping, proposed by Canadian Prime Minister Lester Pearson, who won a Nobel Peace Prize for his efforts on this front. The previously-mentioned further possible reform to the UN is the creation of a United Nations Parliamentary Assembly — such a forum will increase dialogue between states, which could play a key role in diffusing tensions between states while at the same time increasing the active role of the UN.

---

123 Doyle, Michael W., *Ways of War and Peace: Realism, Liberalism, and Socialism* (New York: W.W. Norton, 1997): 302.

The modern world is also forging a path to peace of its own through globalization and the increasing integration of global markets: "the mutually reinforcing dynamics of transnational economic integration, the diffusion of liberal democracy and the growth of international governance creates the conditions for an expanding liberal zone of peace in which war increasingly becomes an irrational or unthinkable instrument of interstate politics."[124] From an economic perspective, "Scholars like Montesquieu, Adam Smith, Richard Cobden, Norman Angell, and Richard Rosecrance have long speculated that free markets have the potential to free states from the looming prospect of recurrent warfare".[125] American political scientists John R. Oneal and Bruce M. Russett state original thinkers "expected democracy and laissez-faire economics to diminish the frequency of war."[126] Immanuel Kant (1724–1804) similarly put forward that, "By virtue of mutual interest does nature unite people against violence and war . . . the spirit of trade cannot coexist with war and sooner or later this spirit dominates every people. For among all those powers . . . that belong to a nation, financial power may be the most reliable in forcing nations to pursue the noble cause of peace . . . and wherever in the world war threatens to break out, they will try to head it off through mediation, just as if they were permanently leagued for this purpose."[127]

Economic integration is only one aspect of liberal theory that has pushed increasingly towards world peace. More directly to the point of peace, we have democratic peace theory. This is a theory which Jack Levy says is "as close as anything we have to

---

124 Russett, Bruce; Oneal, John R., *Triangulating Peace: Democracy, Interdependence, and International Organizations* (W. W. Norton & Company, 2002) from Held, D.; McGrew A., *Governing Globalization: Power, Authority and Global Governance* (Cambridge: Polity Press, 2001): 268.

125 Gartzke, Erik, "Economic Freedom and Peace," in *Economic Freedom of the World: 2005 Annual Report* (Vancouver: Fraser Institute, 2005): 1.

126 Oneal, J. R.; Russet, B. M., "The Classical Liberals Were Right: Democracy, Interdependence, and Conflict, 1950–1985," *International Studies Quarterly* No. 41 (1997): 267–294.

127 Kant, Immanuel, *To Perpetual Peace,* ed. Ted Humphrey, First Supplement, Point 3 (Indianapolis: Hackett Publishing Company, 2003 [1795]): 25.

an empirical law in international relations".[128] Democratic peace theory says democracies are far less likely to have war between themselves than undemocratic states would. This concept extends from the work of Immanuel Kant who said that "if the consent of the citizens is required in order to decide that war should be declared ... nothing is more natural than that they would be very cautious in commencing such a poor game."[129] Economic integration and the growth of democracies around the globe only strengthen the need for a foreign policy based around diplomacy and multilateralism. Such a foreign policy must recognize the individual as well as other states, as is reflected in the concept of human security, which in turn benefits the state by moving towards an end to genocide and terrorism.

Everything a New Liberal stands for inherently relates to the concept of world peace through adopting the policies of federalism and multiculturalism, helping build governance by reducing democratic deficits and expanding the rule of law, providing essential services, being tough on extremists and pursuing nuclear disarmament, all while reaffirming human rights. Empowerment of the individual is the key to achieving world peace, and that empowerment takes place through the provision of adequate health care and education around the globe.

The greatest threats to international peace and security in the 21st Century are those practices which are unsustainable. Being proactive in the areas of climate change, debt levels and inequalities around the globe enhances peace. These three issues more than any other are the greatest reasons for conflict in the modern era. Peace can not only be pursued at the global level but can be sought throughout civil society and the actions of individuals. The greatest freedom is peace and often the greatest way to attaining freedom is through peace — the struggle for freedom has been most powerful when done peacefully. Mohandas Gandhi (1869–1948), who enabled India to become free by utilizing principles

---

128 Levy, Jack S., "Domestic politics and war," *Journal of Interdisciplinary History* Vol. 18, No. 4 (1988): 653–73.

129 Kant, Immanuel, *To Perpetual Peace* translated and reprinted in *On History*, ed. Lewis Beck (New Jersey: Prentice Hall, 1963 [1795]): 94.

of non-violence, is commonly known as 'Mahatma' or 'teacher' as a result. Martin Luther King Jr. worked peacefully for civil rights to be extended to all in the United States of America. Nelson Mandela worked to unite South Africa peacefully while still in jail, then made the country a world leader in human rights.

The entire New Liberal approach is geared towards making a world that is more peaceful and more secure. Thanks to the work of liberalism through history, the world has become more integrated and more political reforms have taken place to guarantee the freedom of individuals. Liberalism has further empowered individuals by strengthening health care and education provisions around the globe. Where these reforms have been implemented, greater peace has flourished. However, these domestic reforms need to be equally met with a global view as provided for under New Liberalism — a strengthening of the United Nations, a return to multilateralism and a focus on human security which can end terrorism, genocide and other crimes against humanity.

Conclusion

New Liberalism is ultimately about protecting our society and our planet. It is about modernizing liberalism to tackle the challenges of today as well as those to come tomorrow. It is about taking the best of our traditions and focusing them on our future. We have seen the state change from the watchman state to the welfare state to the regulatory state and, now, to the post-regulatory state. We have seen the markets go from laissez-faire to Keynesian economics to neoclassical to neo- and New Keynesianism. Throughout this time there has been an increasingly greater pull down to the individual and up to the global level — all of this has been based on liberalism and liberal internationalism.

What we have seen throughout this whole process has been a focus on the individual and the freedom of that individual. This vision has overthrown monarchs, brought millions out of poverty and will hopefully further mitigate the effects of global warming. In each stage of liberalism we have seen an internal modernization that took place in order to serve the needs of society at that time. Liberalism started under the hand of John Locke, broadened in the writings of Hobhouse one hundred years ago and today evolves to a New Liberalism.

While *New Liberalism* has focused on defining the role of the state for the 21st Century, the philosophy presented truly has at its core the concept of individual responsibility — responsibility for yourself, your community and your children and grandchildren. While the state still has a role to protect us from harm and enhance our opportunities in a sustainable fashion, it is the individual who needs to accept responsibility. Responsibility from the individual truly is the precondition for all new liberal policies to work. Without individual responsibility, rights cannot be acquired nor freedom attained.

It is only when individuals internalize this sense of responsibility that rights and freedoms can truly be realized. The concept of freedom has changed throughout history, from negative to positive and now, timeless. Tied to this notion of freedom has been the social contract addressing the amount of power the individual consents to allow the state. This process has consistently demanded greater global infrastructure, including a reformed United Nations, alongside greater empowerment of the individual. The global financial crisis has highlighted a need for a new social contract and a new relationship between the state and markets.

Within the scope of the new social contract and the new relationship with the markets, the role of the state as the enabler of freedom has arisen. The policies it brings forth should meet the three-stage test that is at the heart of New Liberalism. Firstly, does a policy protect people from harm? Secondly, does the policy enhance opportunities? Thirdly, does it leave a better future? These policies need to be implemented by leaders who understand the limits of their powers.

New Liberalism should be seen as a road map to peace. From Adam Smith onwards, we have seen that economic integration pushes us closer and closer to true freedom. With the rise of liberal democracies and political freedoms came more and stronger calls for peace, with liberalism recognizing the route to that goal through democratic peace theory and other concepts that spelled out the essential relationship between peace and freedom.

The twenty-first century holds two potential scenarios — two possible stories to be written by future historians.

In the first scenario, the implications of environmental issues are ignored, global debt and attendant deficits continue to rise and the gap in worldwide social inequality continues to expand. Climate change could lead to mass population migrations as sea levels rise and, as oil supplies are depleted, a growing and increasingly hostile competition to secure scarce resources will be a given. Likewise, growing debt and increasing deficits will lead to deeper global market instability. Barriers to social equality will lead some to terrorism and increase the possibility of armed conflicts.

This scenario holds grave consequences and could severely impact societal stability, both within states and globally. Such conditions have sparked countless wars, civil and international, in the past and likely would again.

The second story is a vastly different one. If action is taken that addresses these pressing matters in conjunction with the establishment of structures that support and empower individual members of society, world peace — a state heretofore elusive to human beings — could become a reality.

We hold in our hands the opportunity to create a better future for ourselves, for our children and for generations to come. However, this is only possible if individuals take greater responsibility for their actions while simultaneously calling for governance that is bold in approach and compassionate in action.

Ultimately, New Liberalism is about peace, order and good government. Each is essential to our collective well-being. Each is essential today more than ever before.

References

Albanese, Patrizia, *Child Poverty in Canada* (Oxford University Press Canada, 2009).

Amnesty International, "Counter-terrorism and criminal law in the EU," (2005).

Angela, Bonnie; Melville, Frank, "An Interview with Thatcher," *Time Magazine* (May 14 1979).

Berlin, Isaiah, "Two Concepts of Liberty," *Four Essays on Liberty* (Oxford: Oxford University Press, 1969).

Berlin, Isaiah, *Liberty: Incorporating Four Essays on Liberty* (Oxford: Oxford University Press, 2002).

Bloom, Alexander, *Prodigal Sons: The New York Intellectuals and Their World* (Oxford: Oxford University Press, 1986).

Bowen, William G.; Davis, Richard G.; Kopf, David H., "The Public Debt: A Burden on Future Generations?" *The American Economic Review* Vol. 50 No. 4 (1960).

Braine, Theresa, "Reaching Mexico's Poorest," *Bulletin of the World Health Organization* (2011).

Centre for Civil Society, "What is civil society?" (London School of Economics, 2004). **http://www.lse.ac.uk/collections/CCS/what_is_civil_society.htm.** Retrieved July 12 2010.

Charter of the United Nations (1945).

Christen, Robert Peck; Rosenberg, Richard; Jayadeva, Veena, *Financial institutions with a double-bottom line: implications for the future of microfinance* (2004) CGAP Occasional Paper.

Chorlton v. Lings [1868] LR 4 CP 374.

"Cycle of Poverty," *The Unabridged Hutchinson Encyclopedia* (Research Machines, 2009).

Dasgupta, Partha, "Positive Freedom, Markets and the Welfare State," *Oxford Review of Economic Policy* Vol. 2 No. 2 (1986).

De Souza v. Cobden [1891] 1 Q.B. 687, at 691, 60 L.J.Q.B. 533.

de Secondat, Charles, Baron de Montesquieu, *The Spirit of the Laws* (Crowder, Wark, and Payne, 1777), 2 vols., originally published anonymously (1748).

Douglas, Roy, *Liberals: A History of the Liberal and Liberal Democrat Parties* (London and New York: Hambledon and London, 2005).

Doyle, Michael W., *Ways of War and Peace: Realism, Liberalism, and Socialism* (New York: W.W. Norton, 1997).

Edwards v. Canada (Attorney General) [1930] AC 124.

Eisenhower, D., *State of the Union Message* (1960).

Friedman, Milton; Friedman, Rose, *Free to Choose: A Personal Statement* (Harcourt Brace Jovanovich, 1980).

Friedman, Thomas, *The World Is Flat: A Brief History of The Twenty-first Century* (Farrar, Straus and Giroux, 2005).

Fukayama, Francis, *The End of History and the Last Man* (Free Press, 1992).

Gartzke, Erik, "Economic Freedom and Peace," in *Economic Freedom of the World: 2005 Annual Report* (Vancouver: Fraser Institute, 2005).

Giddens, Anthony, *The Politics of Climate Change* (Cambridge: Polity Press, 2009).

Giddens, Anthony, *Runaway World: How Globalization is Reshaping Our Lives* (Routledge, 2000).

Giddens, Anthony, *The Third Way: The Renewal of Social Democracy* (Cambridge: Polity Press, 1998).

Gladstone, William, *On the Domestic and Foreign Affairs of England* (1879).

Green, T.H., *Lectures on the Principles of Political Obligation* (Batoche Books, 1883).

Gutman, Leslie Morrison; Sameroff, Arnold J.; Cole, Robert, "Academic Growth Curve Trajectories from 1st Grade to 12th Grade: Effects of Multiple Social Risk Factors and Preschool Child Factors," in *Developmental Psychology* Vol. 39 No. 4 (Jul 2003).

Harvey, D., *A Brief History of Neoliberalism* (University of Chicago Center for International Studies Beyond the Headlines Series, 2005).

Held, David, *Global Covenant: The Social Democratic Alternative to the Washington Consensus* (Polity Press: Cambridge, 2004).

Hobbes, Thomas, *Leviathan* (1651).

Hobhouse, L.T., *Liberalism* (Williams and Norgate, London, 1911).

Hobhouse, L.T., The Elements of Social Justice (H. Holt and company, New York, 1922).
Hughes, Vivien, International Implications of the "Persons" Case (Canadian High Commission, London, 2000). **http://www. collectionscanada.ca/04/0431_e. html.** Retrieved February 20 2006.

International Monetary Fund (IMF) — Mission Statement.
Jackson, Andrew, *First Inaugural Address* (1829).

Jackson, Guy, "World needs new Bretton Woods, says Brown" (Agence France-Presse, 2008).

Janssen, Rodney and the Renewable Energy Working Party, *Renewable Energy . . . into the Mainstream* (International Energy Agency, 2003).

Kalkman, Matthew, "Responsibility To Protect: A Bow Without An Arrow," *Cambridge Student Law Review* Vol. 5, No. 1 (Cambridge, 2009).

Kant, Immanuel, *Perpetual Peace: A Philosophical Sketch* (1795).

Keck, Margaret E.; Sikkink, Kathryn, Activists Beyond Borders: *Advocacy Networks in International Politics* (Ithaca and London: Cornell University Press, 1998).

Keynes, John Maynard, *The General Theory of Employment, Interest and Money* (Palgrave Macmillan, 1936).

Kimmel, Jean, "Child Care, Female Employment, and Economic Growth," *Journal of the Community Development Society*, Vol. 37 No. 2 (Summer 2006). **http://economicdevelopmentandchildcare.org/documents/special_journal_issues/jcds/kimmel.pdf.** Retrieved August 4 2011.

Krugman, Paul, *The Return of Depression Economics and the Crisis of 2008* (W.W. Norton Company Limited, 2009).

Kymlicka, Will, *Multicultural Citizenship: A Liberal Theory of Minority Rights* (Oxford: Oxford University Press, 1996).

Kymlicka, Will, *Politics in the Vernacular: Nationalism, Multiculturalism, Citizenship* (Oxford: Oxford University Press, 2001).

"Legality of the Threat or Use of Nuclear Weapons," Advisory Opinion of 8 July 1996 — General List No. 95 (1995–1998).

Levy, Jack S., http://jstor.org/stable/204819, *Journal of Interdisciplinary History* Vol. 18 No. 4 (1988).

Locke, J., *The Two Treatises of Civil Government* (Hollis, 1689).

Lucio, B., "Civil Society Meets the State: Towards Associational Democracy," *Socio-Economic Review* (2005). **http://ser.oxfordjournals.org/cgi/reprint/mwj031v1.pdf.** Retrieved November 15 2009.

Magna Carta (1215)

Majone, G., "From the Positive to the Regulatory State: Causes and Consequences from Changes in the Modes of Governance," *Journal of Public Policy*, 17 (2) (1997).

Mill, John Stuart, *On Liberty* (London: Longman, Roberts & Green, 1869).

Mill, John Stuart, *Autobiography*. vol.1, ed. J. Robson and J. Stillinger (Toronto: Toronto UP, 1981).

Nairn v. St. Andrew's University [1909] AC 147.

Obama, Barack, *Copenhagen Conference* (2009).

Oneal, J. R.; Russet, B. M., "The Classical Liberals Were Right: Democracy, Interdependence, and Conflict, 1950–1985," *International Studies Quarterly* 41 (1997).

Pellegrino, Charles R., *The Last Train from Hiroshima: The Survivors Look Back* (New York: Henry Holt and Co., 2010).

Pimlott, Daniel, "Q & A on Tobin tax," *The Financial Times* (November 8 2009). **http://www.ft.com/cms/s/0/8e68678a-ccba-11de-8e30-00144feabdc0.html**. Retrieved February 10 2010.

Princen, T., Finger, M., Manno, J.P., "Translational linkages," in Princen, T.; Finger, M. (eds.), *Environmental NGOs in World Politics: Linking the Local and the Global* (Routledge, London, 1994).

Quesnay, F., "Tableau économique" from Spiegel, Henry William (1983) *The Growth of Economic Thought*, Revised and Expanded Edition (Duke University Press, 1759).

Rawls, J., *A Theory of Justice* (Cambridge, Massachusetts: Belknap Press of Harvard University Press, 1971).

Reagan, Ronald, *First Inaugural Address* (1981).

Viscountess Rhondda's Claim [1922] 2 AC 339.

Riley, Maude, "Outcome — Women are 'Persons.'" **http://www.famous5.org/frames/frame_educationresearch.htm**. Retrieved February 21 2006.

Riley, Naomi Schaefer, "Mr. Compassionate Conservatism," *The Wall Street Journal* (October 21 2006).

Robbins, M W, ed.,. "Japanese Engineer Survived Atomic Strike on Hiroshima and Nagasaki," *Military History Magazine* (Weider History Group, August/September 2009).

Roubini, Nouriel, *Why Central Banks Should Burst Bubbles* (Stern School of Business, NYU, 2005).

Rousseau, Jean-Jacques, *The Social Contract, or Principles of Political Right* (1762).

Russett, Bruce; Oneal, John R., *Triangulating Peace: Democracy, Interdependence, and International Organizations* (W. W. Norton & Company, 2002) from Held, D.; McGrew A., *Governing Globalization: Power, Authority and Global Governance* (Cambridge: Polity Press, 2001).

Schlesinger, Jr., Arthur, "Liberalism in America: A Note for Europeans" (1956) from *The Politics of Hope* (Boston: Riverside Press, 1962).

Sen, Amartya "Food and Freedom," Sir John Crawford Memorial Lecture, Washington (1987).

Smith, Adam, *The Theory of Moral Sentiments,* ed. D.D. Raphael and A.L. Macfie, vol. 1 of *The Glasgow Edition of the Works and Correspondence of Adam Smith* (Indianapolis: Liberty Fund, 1982 [1759]).

Smith, Adam, *The Wealth of Nations* (Oxford: Clarendon Press, 1979).

Social Insurance and Allied Services (Beveridge Report, 1942).

"Stiglitz Recommendations," *CNN* (September 17 2008). **http://www.cnn.com/2008/POLITICS/09/17/stiglitz.crisis/index.html.** Retrieved June 20 2010.

"The Economist-Rajan-Cycle Proof Regulation," *The Economist* (April 8 2009). **http://www.economist.com/finance/displaystory.cfm?story_id=13446173.** Retrieved July 21 2010.

Thoreau, Henry David, *Resistance to Civil Government* (Civil Disobedience, 1849).

Uchitelle, Louis, "Glass-Steagall vs. the Volcker Rule", *The New York Times* (January 22 2010). **http://economix.blogs.nytimes.com/2010/01/22/glass-steagall-vs-the-volcker-rule/.** Retrieved February 15 2010.

United States Declaration of Independence (1776).

US Department of Defense, "Joint Publication 1-02 Department of Defense Dictionary of Military and Associated Terms" (12 July 2007).

UNFCCC (2009) Copenhagen Accord. Draft decision -/CP.15, FCCC/CP/2009/L.7 [electronic version] **unfccc.int/resource/docs/2009/cop15/eng/l07.pdf.** Retrieved December 25 2010.

UNICEF *State of the World's Children 2005: Childhood Under Threat* (UNICEF, 2005).

United Nations, "Report of the World Commission on Environment and Development," General Assembly Resolution 42/187 (December 11 1987).

United Nations International Convention for the Suppression of Acts of Nuclear Terrorism (Nuclear Terrorism Convention, 2005).

Vasak, Karel, "Human Rights: A Thirty-Year Struggle: the Sustained Efforts to give Force of law to the Universal Declaration of Human Rights," *UNESCO Courier* 30:11, (Paris: United Nations Educational, Scientific, and Cultural Organization, 1977).

Wempe, Ben, T.H. *Green's Theory of Positive Freedom* (Imprint Academic, 2004).

"What is the Third Way?" BBC News (September 27 1999).

Wilson, Woodrow, *Fourteen Points*, Joint Session of Congress (1918).

World Commission on Environment and Development, *Our Common Future* (Oxford: Oxford University Press, 1987).

Index

Matthew Kalkman was born in Vancouver in 1988. He has an LL.B. from Durham University and an MSc. from the London School of Economics and Political Science where his studies in regulation focused on the financial crisis and climate change. Furthermore, he represented the LSE as a delegate at the 2009 United Nations Climate Change Conference in Copenhagen.

His writings on the responsibility to protect and the financial crisis have been published in the *Cambridge Student Law Review* and the *Inter Alia Law Journal*, respectively. After a year taking French Language Studies at Laval University in Quebec City, Kalkman has returned to Vancouver to work in environmental law.